Ketogenic Diet for Beginners

Easy 123 Recipes and 2 Weeks Diet Plan

Green Protein

Table of Contents

Chapter Four: Breakfast   38

Chapter Five: Lunch   87

Chapter Seven: Soup 174

Chapter Eight: Snacks 190

Chapter Nine: Drinks 202

Introduction

When it comes to diets and dieting, there are so many diets out there on the market that they're probably making your head spin trying to figure out which one is the best to do and which one will give you the best results. The truth is that when looking at a diet, you need to look at your habits as well as the way you look at food in general. When it comes to foods, there are a few laws that you need to remember and follow.

The first law is that there are no bad foods. When it comes to foods, people like to label them both good and bad. When it comes to food, it is all about quantity and frequency of the foods that we eat. For example, if you were to eat five pounds of chocolate a day your body would take what made up this chocolate and use what it could for energy and store the rest as fat. The same is true if you eat fruits and vegetables at every meal. Your body would soon adapt and react to this and begin drawing from other resources to get what it needs.

When starting a diet, you need to look at it as a lifestyle change and not a quick solution to lose weight. When we structure ourselves with healthy eating habits, we are giving our bodies the tools and resources it needs to function properly.

In this book, we will discuss the Ketogenic diet. We will make you the good and bad points to this diet as well as what you need to take full advantage of its benefits. At the end of this book, you will have the foundation necessary to start developing your meal plans as well as 123 quick and easy recipes that you can use to start eating healthy on the ketogenic meal plan.

Chapter One: Ketogenic Diet 101

When it comes to diets and dieting many people will choose to go on different diets for different reasons. Some people go on diets to lose weight, and others go on diets to boost energy or even increase testosterone levels in the body. Some people go on diets to improve the complexion of their skin while others just go on diets as a lifestyle change or even personal or religious beliefs.

When it comes to the Ketogenic diet those who originally consumed the diet suffered from seizures and other neurological conditions. It was found in several research studies in the 1920's that some foods helped to reduce the onset of seizures as well as other neurological conditions.

When looking at the Ketogenic diet, it has been riddled with controversy since it is a diet high in fat content and for those looking to lose weight the notion that they need to avoid fat is a strong one. The misconception many people have is that all fat is bad for you. They feel if you consume fat it will be broken down by the body and deposited in our arteries as well as the heart which will result in a broad range of health issues later in life.

The fact is that as humans we need fat in our diets. If we fail to consume fat, we will be unable to function. The trick to this is to eat healthy, lean fats that when broken down will help benefit our bodies and not cause long-term health issues.

So what exactly is the Ketogenic Diet?

Well, the Ketogenic Diet or "Keto Diet" for short is high protein, low carbohydrate diet that has been proven to have long-lasting health benefits for those who suffer from extreme weight gain as well as many health effects from being overweight such as cancers, Alzheimer's and diabetes.

When it comes to the Keto diet, the entire goal is to recharge your metabolism. When we consume food, our metabolism is the main powerhouse that breaks down the foods that we eat to create energy. When we have a high metabolism rate the food we consume is transformed directly into energy. If on the other hand if the food that we consume is not broken down into energy due to a slow metabolism, then we are just compounding fat on top of fat which is counter productive.

Getting Started

Before you get started on the Ketogenic diet there is a few things hat you will need to learn. First of all, you will need to go through a detox process. In this detox process, you may feel nauseous, have headaches and just not feel right all over. If this is the case, this is normal. It is something that you will have to work through since it is your body's natural way of adjusting to the lack of carbs, fats, sugars and other foods that you have consumed in the past. This feeling will last about a week or so and once it is over you will be on your way to a healthier lifestyle.

Cutting foods from your diet

The next thing that you will need to know is that you will need to cut certain foods from your diet. Now many of you might think that this is a deal breaker, but if you are serious about loosing weight and eating a healthy lifestyle, you need to take these foods out of our diet and keep them out.

When it comes to the Ketogenic diet, it is not something that you can start tomorrow. You will need to mentally prepare yourself as well as physically prepare yourself for what is to come. If you don't then you will fail and fall back into your old eating habits.

Dairy in the Diet

Before committing yourself to going forward with the ketogenic diet, you will need to know that dairy and dairy products play a huge role in keto. For many people consuming dairy may be a problem due to lactose intolerance or their personal beliefs when it comes to consuming foods from animals. If you are someone who has a concern when it comes to dairy, then keto may not be the diet for you. If you do like dairy and dairy products, you want to try and keep your dairy intake to 4 ounces a day.

Setting your Body Foundation

When it comes to getting started on the Keto diet, you need to fist stabilize yourself and your body. The reason for this is that your body is currently consuming glucose as fuel. Glucose is what your body turns your food into to use as energy. If you don't use all of your glucose, your body will transform the remaining glucose into fat and store it in your body for later consumption.

When we reset our bodies, we are now setting ourselves up to deplete the stored glucose as well as the glucose that we consume as energy. Once this is accomplished, we can then focus our body's energy towards the stored fat that we have as its source of fuel. If we don't do this, then we will continue to fight this cycle adding more and more fat to our bodies and stop the weight loss cycle altogether. When first starting out on the ketogenic diet we want to consume the following amounts in our diets.

Protein – 20%
Carbs – 5%
Fats - 75%

Another thing that you don't want to worry about is number of calories that you are consuming. When it comes to resetting our bodies, the calories don't matter at this point but will later in the process. Bur, for now, focus on these numbers to set a baseline.

People who should focus on the ketogenic diet

When it comes to the Ketogenic diet, there are a few groups of people who should consider it. The first group is those who have a high risk of cancer. When we have cancer or if cancer is something that is prominent in your family you will want to consider going on the Ketogenic diet. It has been shown that those who go on the ketogenic diet have lessened their risk as well as seen dramatic reductions in cancers that they have already acquired.

Help reduce or eliminate diabetes

When it comes to diabetes and type two diabetes, many doctors contribute this condition to the diet that we consume. If you are someone who has diabetes either border line, type one or type two, it is important that you turn to the ketogenic diet. It has been shown that those who have gone on the ketogenic diet have decreased their risk of diabetes and even reverse the condition altogether.

Weight Loss

When it comes to this diet, many people who need to lose weight have tried all of the other diets on the market and have found that the ketogenic diet has done the trick for them. The main thing that you need to realize though is that the ketogenic diet is not a quick fix and that it is a lifestyle change more than a simple jump on and jump off a diet. If you decide to go on the ketogenic diet, it is a lifelong commitment and should be considered as such.

Alzheimer's disease

When the diet was first introduced, it was quickly discovered that it helped people suffering from seizures. After additional studies were conducted those who were at risk or who were suffering from Alzheimer's disease benefited greatly from this diet. If you or someone you know is at risk of this disease switching to the ketogenic diet will have short-term as well as long-term benefits.

When it comes to the ketogenic diet, this is the basic foundation that you need to know. In the next chapter we are going to dive into the diet itself and talk about the foods that you can eat, what you can't eat and exactly what you can expect from starting and maintaining the ketogenic diet.

Chapter Two: All You Can Learn

Now that you have a basic foundation of what the Ketogenic diet is and why it is so useful it is time to dive deep into the diet itself and learn the foundation. First of all, when going on this diet, you will be able to eat the majority of the foods that you consume now. The major difference in the foods is the portions and the specific sources of the food you eat. Let's break it down into its simplest forms.

Fats

When we hear the word fat many of us will cringe. We hear the word fat and immediately hear the world unhealthy or bad for you. When it comes to fats, we need to realize that there are two types of fats. There are good fats, and there are bad fats. When it comes to the ketogenic diet, we are going to focus on the good fats.

What are good fats?

Good fats are the fats that occur naturally in the foods that we eat. These fats are easily broken down in the body and are used as the foundation for the fuel our bodies use as energy. When we look at the good fat foods, we are looking at foods such as Eggs, Avocados, nuts, fish and other healthy foods choices along those lines. When we look at these fats, they are produced by the natural oils of these foods and contain vitamins and minerals such as omega-3 fatty acids.

When it comes to bad fats, these are the fats that we want to avoid. The number one bad fat that you want to avoid are Trans-Fats. These are the fats that manufacturers put into their foods to give them a longer shelf life. These fats, when consumed by the body, will only do harm as they remain in the body setting the foundation for long-term health issues.

Proteins

The next thing that you will need to look at when it comes to the ketogenic diet is your proteins. When it comes to proteins, these are the building blocks for our entire body. It is vital that we consume lean, healthy proteins on a daily basis to build our muscles as well as other areas of our bodies. If we fail to consume healthy amounts of proteins, then our bodies will not have what it needs to build upon itself.

Lean Proteins

The first classification of proteins that you will want to consume will be fish such as tuna, fowl such as chicken and turkey and lean meat such as beef and pork. Now for many people, they consider these to be fatty and not good for you, but in fact, they are very healthy if you choose the correct cut of meat and cook it with healthy oil or baked in the oven. Adding in additional fats will make these foods unhealthy but they are healthy in their base forms.

Fatty proteins

When it comes to fat, you may want to consider adding in these foods in conjunction with your regular fat intake. These fats that are included in these proteins are also healthy for you. These fatty protein foods include eggs, several different cuts of red meat, dairy foods such as cottage cheese as well as some forms of fresh fish.

Dairy

As mentioned earlier dairy is one of those controversial foods that are included in the ketogenic diet. When it comes to dairy, many people may have an adverse reaction and may feel bloated and weighed down. If this is the case, you may want to play with the different foods that contain dairy as well as the proteins and fats you need to boost your metabolism.

Carbs

Now, this is a topic that everyone will be interested in. When it comes to carbs or carbohydrates in our diets, many doctors and health professionals will say that you need to remove carbs from your diet. Well, this is a mistake. When it comes to carbs, you need them to form a full balanced diet. The trick is to only have carbs or low carb foods on a part-time basis to get the benefits without all the problems.

When it comes to carbs, you will want to have bread, pasta, and rice. These are known as the low carb or gluten foods. You will also want to have fresh vegetables. When we consume vegetables, we are consuming vitamins and minerals that our bodies need. We are also consuming natural sugars that our body also uses to convert into glucose for energy.

The carbs that we want to avoid are those that contain a lot of sugar or have sugars added to them. When we eat foods that have natural sugars in them, our bodies are taking in just the right amount and are not being overwhelmed with added sugars that it will turn into fat. When we add sugar to our foods, we are just adding a psychological taste to our bodies that our minds enjoy, but our bodies will pay for later. So look for some sugars that are added to your foods and try to stay with the natural sugars for that much-needed sweetness we all crave.

From here we now have the basis for the entire ketogenic diet. In the next chapter, we will begin to develop a meal plan that you can follow to start gaining the much-needed benefits from the diet and start seeing results from these efforts.

Shopping List Guide

When it comes to shopping for the ketogenic diet here is a list of items that you will want to have on hand in your home:

	Asparagus	Avocado
Beef	Bell Pepper Green	Broccoli
Butter Head Lettuce	Carrots Baby	Catfish
Cauliflower	Celery	Chicken
Clams	Cod	Crab
Cucumber	Duck	Flounder
Garlic	Goat	Green Beans
Halibut	Ham	Lamb
Lobster	Mackerel	Mahi-Mahi
Mushrooms Button	Mussels	Onion Green
Onion White	Oysters	Peanut Butter
Pheasant	Pickles Dill	Pork Chops
Pork Loin	Quail	Romaine Lettuce
Salmon	Scallops	Shallots
Snapper	Snow Peas	Spinach
Squash Acorn	Squash Butternut	Squash Spaghetti
Squid	Tomato	Trout
Tuna	Veal	Whole Eggs

Chapter Three: Ketogenic Diet Plan

In this chapter, we will set the foundation for a healthy ketogenic diet plan. From this plan, you will be able to adjust and make corrections to better benefit your ultimate results.

When it comes to making a meal plan the first thing that I want you to do is to make a list of the foods that you love, the foods you hate and the foods that you should give up to live a healthier lifestyle. The main purpose of this exercise is to learn about the foods that you eat and why you eat them. Many people don't look at the foods that they eat. Many people will choose the foods that they eat based on an emotional connection rather than a health-based choice.

When we were young children, our parents and grandparents would tell us to sit down and eat our vegetables, eat everything that was on our plate and drink lots of water and milk. Then after these meals, they would sit us down in front of the television and stuff us with sweets such as candy, cookies, and chocolates. This style of eating sent mixed messages as to the quality and the purpose of food.

When we were sick or not feeling well on a physical or an emotional level our parents and grandparents would give us what is known as comfort food which in many cases was filled with sugars, preservatives and other chemicals that reacted in a pleasurable way on our brains but in a negative way on our bodies. When we became adults, we associated these foods with healthy eating since our doctors say we are the picture of health.

When it comes to dieting and eating healthy, we need to break out of this mindset and move more towards developing eating plans and habits that are more conducive to our bodies needs at this stage in life. This is why I want you to break down the foods that you eat and why.

The Foods That You Love

What are the foods that you love? Make a list of the foods that you love and the reasons behind them. This doesn't have to be complicated writing down things such as Chocolate because it tastes good, Pizza because it is cheap and easy, and continue with this process until you have a list of the most common foods that you eat on a consistent basis.

Foods that you can give up

Once you have the list completed go back and read through your list. I want you to cross off everything on that list except for five foods. These five foods will be the only thing that you can eat as your cheat foods on the keto diet.

The Foods Don't Like

The next thing I want you to do is to repeat the process, but instead of writing down the foods that you love I want you to write down the foods that you don't like eating and why. This can be anything that is healthy for you. Don't write down foods that are unhealthy since adding unhealthy foods to your diet is counterproductive. The majority of the foods that you write in this list will be foods that are right for you, that you don't like to eat and why.

Developing a Meal Plan

Now that you have gone through all of the foods that you like to eat and all of the foods that you don't like you can begin to paint a picture of how you can construct your own ketogenic meal plan. In the next chapter, I am going to give you *one hundred and twenty-three* great tasting recipes that you can try and experiment with. Feel free to substitute some of your healthy favorites with different parts of the recipes as long as they fall within the ketogenic guidelines. In the next section, you will find a sample meal plan that you can follow and adjust to your specific needs.

2 Weeks Ketogenic Diet Plan

Week 1

In the first week, we will begin to condition your body to start losing weight. You will want to follow this diet closely and not deviate too much if not at all. If you make changes, then you may see skewed results.

Day #1 – To start off our diet I decided to give you a plan that would wet your whistle as well as give you a basic idea of what to expect when jumping into to the ketogenic diet. For breakfast I want you to have a belly-filling bowl of porridge.   This will put some meat on your ribs like my mom used to say and keep you energized for your morning activities.

For lunch, I wanted to keep it a more traditional with a bacon burger. Make sure to keep off the cheese and drop the bun to keep it keto, but the burger is an excellent way to ease your way into the diet.

For dinner, I wanted to round you out with some of my favorite meals so I decided that for a treat you can have some mouth watering ribs. Yummy.

For desert I want you to have a little bit of what you missed on your burger, so this is why I decided on the mozzarella bites. These go great to snack on when sitting in front of the television watching a movie with your family.

Breakfast – Hemp Heart Porridge
Lunch – Bunless Bacon Burger
Dinner – Ribs

Desert - Mozzarella Bites

Day #2 – On day two I am going to give you some more favorites but start to add in some extras. We start out with the spinach and sausage frittata. These are great and easy to make in the morning.

For lunch, I wanted to go light but give you some substance. This is why a steak salad is great and will keep you motivated.

Dinner is simple with some meatballs. You can start this in the morning and let them cook all day. When you get home from your long day, you can just plate them up and go.

For your desert, I wanted to add in fruit, so this is why I decided on the raspberry Popsicle. A little ice cream type dessert will help clean your palate from the meatballs and give you a soothing pop or flavor from the raspberries.

Breakfast – Spinach, Sausage & Feta Frittata
Lunch – Steak Salad
Dinner – Crock Pot Meatballs
Dessert - Raspberry Popsicles

Day #3 – For today I wanted to show you that you can reuse meats that you have for multiple meals. This is why I chose to do chicken. For breakfast I want you to do something light like the keto cereal.

It will fill you up but not be too heavy. Next for lunch keep your metabolism running and burning fat just by adding a little fuel to the chicken and walnut salad.

For dinner, you can use up the rest of the chicken you had for lunch and make yourself a small personalized pan pizza with the chicken and bbq sauce. I love chicken on my pizza and would eat this all day if I could

For dessert, I decided to knock the chicken out of the park with the corndog bites. These are great to snack on if you are fighting hunger pains and can be taken with you if you are out on the town or just sitting home with the family.

Breakfast – Keto Cereal
Lunch – Chicken Salad with Walnuts
Dinner – Barbeque Chicken Pizza
Desert – Corndog Bites

Day #4 – For today I wanted to give you a light meal so that your body will have fuel and start munching away at your fat. For breakfast, you can start with a simple egg porridge and then have a stuffed avocado for lunch. The avocado is considered one of those super foods so combining them with the protein of the egg will kick start your system into fat burning mode.

For dinner, I choose chicken nuggets since they were filling and could be made quickly. And for dessert, you can have the veggies to get your sugars and extra fuel for burning that fat.

Breakfast – Egg Porridge
Lunch – Stuffed Avocado
Dinner – Chicken Nuggets
Desert – Veggie Dip

Day #5 – On day five I want to give you a little treat in the morning with pumpkin pancakes. Pumpkin is an excellent vegetable as well as smells great. Having some pancakes in the morning will remind you of your childhood and fill your stomach for the day ahead.

For lunch, a smoked chicken salad will give you protein as well as the veggies you need to get through your day. It will also be light helping to improve your metabolism.

For dinner, a light meat such as pork will taste great as well as keep away those unwanted saturated fats. And finally, go to bed with one of the world's best superfoods attacking your fat cells while you sleep with the avocado smoothie for desert.

Breakfast – Pumpkin Pancakes
Lunch – Smoked Chicken Salad
Dinner – Creamy Pork Loin

Desert – Avocado Smoothie

Day #6 – We're almost done with the first week of your keto diet, and on this day I wanted to give you another kick start on the diet. For breakfast, you will want to start with the granola to get those proteins and vitamins into your system. Then the chicken chowder will fill you up and keep you moving through the rest of your day.

For dinner a treat with the bacon stir fry. This will remind you that there are good old meals that are bad for you in your mind. And finally, wash away the bacon badness with some strawberry goodness with the strawberry smoothie. Bacon and ice cream in one day. Yummy to the max!

Breakfast – Grain-Free Granola
Lunch – Crock Pot Chicken Chowder
Dinner – Bacon Stir Fry
Dessert - Strawberries Smoothie

Day #7 – The first week is at an end, and I wanted to give you a great meal to fill you up and have some fun. First of all, lets start off with that great superfood again the avocado. It will give you some fuel for the day and start working on those fat cells. For lunch, you can go out with your friends and have a delicious Stromboli. Then when you get home to have some amazing chicken spaghetti which will fill you up and keep you satisfied. And to wash it all down a berry smoothie to help break up your foods and prepare you for the next exciting week.

Breakfast – Best Avocado Breakfast
Lunch – Stromboli
Dinner – Chicken Spaghetti
Desert - Berry Smoothie

Week #2

Well, you are half way there. You have made it through your first week on the keto diet and should be raring to go for week number two. In this week I wanted to push your system into really burning that fat and showing results. I hope that my meal choices will keep you motivated and ready for action.

Day #1 – On the first day of the new week I wanted to keep your meal simple. Starting off with some breakfast hash to give you fuel to get you started for the day. Then for lunch something quick and easy that will give you some extra boost. The stuffed banana peppers will be great. Peppers have a lot of natural fat burning power and banana peppers have that extra pop of flavor that will keep you wanting more.

For dinner I wanted to keep your meats lean again so frying up some pork chops in healthy oil will give you the protein and satisfaction you have been looking for. For dessert, a simple nut mix will suffice. Nothing too heavy but something to munch on when those cravings hit.

Breakfast – Breakfast Hash
Lunch – Stuffed Banana Peppers
Dinner – Fried Pork Chops
Desert - Nut Mix

Day #2 – For breakfast today I wanted to give you a little twist. Many people think of having ham and eggs, but for today on your keto diet, I am giving you fish and eggs. Fish is great and with the essential fish oils contained within you are doing great things for your hair and skin.

For lunch, I wanted to give you a little bit of normality. This is where the pizza comes in. There is nothing like going on a diet and being able to take a bite into a nice slice of pizza. With this pizza, you are not only satisfying your physical health but your mental health as well.

To move away from the sinful pizza, you will want to have a nice clean meat again to flush out your system. Pork is a clean and tasty meat and should be one of your friends this far into the two-week diet.

For desert something cool and refreshing. Cucumber chips will give you something too much on while flushing out your system of any unwanted toxins.

Breakfast – Fish and Egg Breakfast
Lunch – Alfredo Pizza
Dinner – Pork Kabobs
Desert - Cucumber Chips

Day #3 – Day three is a great day as well. It is going to be a nice light meal day with some great food choices to keep you moving. For breakfast, you can have the tomato shakshuka. This is a great start for the morning and will give you some much-needed vegetables.

For lunch, you can relive the picnic days with this twist on the traditional deviled eggs. These are so good I can't even believe I made you wait this long in the diet to try them. For dinner, I want to give you a treat so no more pork. Today you can have beef. Here is a great compliment to your lunch. The cheeseburger casserole. For your dessert, I wanted to round out the theme of our childhood memories. The peanut butter log is quick simple and will remind you of those good old days of when you could eat anything and still not gain an ounce.

Breakfast – Tomato Shakshuka

Lunch – Chicken Salad Deviled Eggs

Dinner – Cheeseburger Casserole

Desert – Peanut Butter Log

Day #4 – Today I wanted to give you the best of both worlds. For breakfast, you can have the simple Cheddar Soufflés which will fill your stomach as well as give you that morning fuel. Then for lunch, you can have a treat with the garlic parmesan wings. The day of mental cheating continues with your dinner of chuck steak and for dessert if you can still handle it the no bake bombs. Yummy.

Breakfast – Cheddar Soufflés

Lunch – Garlic Parmesan Wings

Dinner – Slow Cooked Chuck Steak

Desert – No Bake Bombs

Day #5 – For today I wanted to give you another simple meal. Something to recover from yesterday's fun fest. Today, start out with some simple eggs benedict to build up your fuel reserves. Next, go and try some lemon pepper chicken which will put a smile on your face. For dinner, I wanted to try something new so the moussaka fit the bill quite nicely and finally to curb any hunger pains that you may be feeling go ahead and have some dried fruit mix to cut the edge and have a great night's sleep.

Breakfast – Eggs Benedict

Lunch – Pulled Lemon Pepper Chicken

Dinner – Moussaka

Desert – Dried Fruit Mix

Day #6 – Two days to go and for today I wanted to give you a teeter totter meal plan First off we will start with some sausage and cheese muffins. These are great popping warm out of the oven. Next, for lunch, we will calm it down a little with the cucumber sandwich. Something that will cut that hunger edge left over from the sausage. For dinner, we are going back up on the totter with some great burger bites. These are quick and simple and will fill you up. And finally, if you are still hungry you can come back down with a quick turkey roll-up to munch on for a quick on the go snack.

Breakfast – Sausage and Cheese Muffins

Lunch – Cucumber Sandwich

Dinner – Burger Boats

Desert - Turkey Roll-up

Day #7 – For your final day on the two-week ketogenic diet I wanted to give you something to remember it by and hopefully keep you coming back to this diet again and again or even transforming the way you eat forever. For breakfast, I wanted to give you a full belly send off with the squash breakfast casserole. This is a great meal you can make the night before and will be even better the next day.

For lunch a nice turkey pesto to clear your palate for the anticipation of your final great meal of the week. For dinner ladies and gentleman, we are going to end it off with steak. Yes, I know you have been chomping down on pork all week and being able to have a nice juicy steak is the only way to end a diet. With the steak pinwheels, you get the best of both worlds. Great tasting meat and steak!

And for dessert, I decided to give you something a little different to show that you don't need those greasy potato chips anymore. These flaxseed chips are great tasting and good for you.

Breakfast – Squash Breakfast Casserole
Lunch – Turkey Pesto
Dinner – Steak Pinwheels
Desert - Flaxseed Chips

Well, there is your meal plan ladies and gentleman. For the past two weeks, you have been eating healthy as well as great tasting meals. In the next chapter, you will be able to find out how to make these great meals on the diet plan as well as several others that you may want to substitute with.

Remember when it comes to going on a diet and changing the way that you eat there is no rule you can't eat good tasting foods. With this meal plan and the recipes that follow I hope that you will do just that. Enjoy!

Chapter Four: Breakfast

1-Spinach, Sausage & Feta Frittata

Total Time: 60 Minutes

Serves: 9 (2-muffins)

Ingredients

- 10 oz. spinach, frozen, thawed, drained, and chopped
- 12 oz. sausage
- ½ cup Feta cheese, crumbled
- 12 eggs
- ½ cup heavy cream
- ½ cup almond milk, unsweetened
- ½ tsp. salt
- ¼ tsp. black pepper
- ¼ tsp. ground nutmeg

Cooking Directions

1. Slice the raw sausage into small pieces, and place them in a medium-sized bowl.
2. Ensure that the spinach is squeezed-dry from any remaining liquid after washing. Break the spinach up into the same bowl as the sausage.
3. Sprinkle feta cheese over the mixture. Toss lightly until fully combined. Lightly spread the mixture onto a greased 13" × 9" casserole dish, or 18 greased muffin cups.

4. In a larger bowl, combine almond milk, cream, nutmeg, salt and pepper with the beaten the eggs together, and mix until well blended.
5. Gently pour the mixture into the dish or muffin cups until for about ¾ full.
6. Bake at 375°F for about 50 minutes (for the casserole), or 30 minutes (for the muffin cups), or until fully set. Serve warm or at room temperature.

Nutritional Value (Amount Per Serving): Calories **295**, Total Fat **24.1**g, Cholesterol **267**mg, Carbohydrate **2.9**g, Fiber **1g**, Protein **17.3**g

2-Coffee Breakfast Pudding

Total Time: 35 Minutes

Serves: 2

Ingredients

- 2 Tbsp. of Herbal Coffee
- 45g of Chai Seeds, Dried
- ⅓ cup of coconut cream, undiluted
- 1 Tbsp. of organic vanilla extract
- 1 packet sweetener (Swerve)
- 30g of Cacao Nibs

Cooking Directions

1. Use two cups of water and add 2 tablespoons of herbal coffee. Let simmer for about 15 minutes or until the liquid approximately measures to 1 cup.
2. Strain out the herbal coffee and add in the Swerve, coconut cream, and vanilla. Blend until smooth.
3. Add the Cacao Nibs and Chai seeds, mixing well.
4. Chill in the refrigerator for 30 minutes.
5. Remove from fridge and serve. If desired, you may add more herbal coffee and cacao nibs on top for decoration and extra flavor.

Nutritional Value (Amount Per Serving): Calories **347**, Total Fat **24.5**g, Cholesterol **0**mg, Carbohydrate **24.3**g, Fiber **12.8**g, Protein **6.3**g

3-Hemp Heart Porridge

Total Time: 5 Minutes

Serves: 1

Ingredients

- 1 cup of Milk Alternative
- 64g of Hemp Hearts
- 2 Tbsps. of ground flax seeds
- 1 Tablespoon of Chia Seeds
- 4g of Xylitol
- ¾ tsp. of pure vanilla extract
- ½ tsp. of ground cinnamon
- ¼ cup almonds, crushed

For the toppings:

- 15g Brazil nuts
- 15g Hemp Hearts

Cooking Directions

1. In a small saucepan, mix all ingredients except the almonds and the toppings.
2. On medium heat, bring the mixture to a light boil.
3. Once boiling leave to cook for another 2 minutes.
4. Remove it from the heat; add the crushed almonds or almond flour.
5. Serve into a bowl and add the toppings.

Nutritional Value (Amount Per Serving): Calories **975**, Total Fat **32.2**g, Cholesterol **0**mg, Carbohydrate **173.9**g, Fiber **9.8g**, Protein **19.1**g

4-Keto Cereal

Total Time: 15 minutes

Serves: 2

Ingredients

- 3 to 4 teaspoons of butter
- ½ cup of coconut, unsweetened and shredded
- 2 cups of flaxseed
- 2g sweetener (optional)
- A dash of salt
- ⅓ cup of crushed walnuts
- ⅓ cup of crushed macadamia nuts

Cooking Directions

1. Toast your nuts and shredded coconut in the oven until reaching the desired flavor.
2. In a pot, melt the butter over medium heat.
3. Add the nuts and salt to the pot, stirring quickly for 2 minutes.
4. Add the coconut; keep stirring to avoid burning the bottom.
5. Add in your sweetener and the milk.
6. Turn off heat and stir for 1 minute more.
7. Serve warm or let it soak for 10 minutes.

Nutritional Value (Amount Per Serving): Calories **1,002**, Total Fat **76.8**g, Cholesterol **15**mg, Carbohydrate **41.4**g, Fiber **36.1**g, Protein **28.3**g

5-Egg Porridge

Total Time: 10 minutes

Serves: 1

Ingredients

- 2 eggs
- ⅓ cup of heavy cream
- 1 packet Sweetener
- 2 Tbsps. of butter
- 1 Tbsp. Ground cinnamon (for taste)

Cooking Directions

1. In a small bowl, whisk together the eggs, cream, and sweetener.
2. In a medium saucepan, melt the butter on medium-high heat. Do not let the butter brown. Once the butter is melted turn heat to low.
3. Add in your egg mixture. Continually mix along the bottom while it thickens and begins to curdle.
4. When the curling has begun to take from heat. The mixture should still be creamy.
5. Serve with plenty of cinnamon sprinkled on top.

Nutritional Value (Amount Per Serving): Calories **484**, Total Fat **46.7**g, Cholesterol **443**mg, Carbohydrate **9.3**g, Fiber **4.6**g, Protein **12.4**g

6-Cream Cheese Pancakes

Total Time: 20 minutes

Serves: 4 6in pancakes

Ingredients

- 2 oz. of cream cheese
- 2 eggs
- 1 tsp. sweetener of choice
- ½ tsp. of ground cinnamon

Cooking Directions

1. Mix all the ingredients in a blender or with an electric mixer. Blend until smooth.
2. Let settle for 2 minutes.
3. Pour the desired amount on a skillet or pan to create pancake.
4. Brown on one side then flip and brown the other side.
5. Remove from skillet and serve with desired topping (syrup, berries, jam).

Nutritional Value (Amount Per Serving): Calories **82**, Total Fat **7.1**g, Cholesterol **97**mg, Carbohydrate **1.3**g, Fiber **0**g, Protein **3.8**g

7-Coconut Flour Pancakes

Total Time: 20 minutes

Serves: 12

Ingredients

- ½ cup of Coconut Flour
- ⅓ cup of coconut, sweetened and shredded
- 32g sweetener
- ½ tsp. baking powder
- ½ tsp. salt
- 6 eggs
- ¼ cup of coconut oil, melted
- 1 cup of almond milk, unsweetened
- 1 tsp. of almond extract
- ¼ cup of almonds, slivered and toasted
- 2 oz. chocolate (cacao), finely chopped

Cooking Directions

1. In a large mixing bowl combine coconut flour, shredded coconut, sweetener, baking powder, and salt.
2. Add in the eggs, oil, and milk as needed. Coconut flour makes the batter thicker than normal pancakes mixes. Make sure not to make it too thick; you should still be able to pour the batter. If settled too long you can add more milk to thin out the batter.
3. Add in the toasted almond and cacao.
4. Heat you pan or skillet to medium heat.
5. Use 2 heaping Tablespoons to create 4in pancakes.

6. Cook until the bottom is golden brown and the edges look dry. Bubbles should be appearing on top. Flip the pancake and brown the other side.
7. Repeat process until you are out of batter.
8. Serve with preferred toppings.

Nutritional Value (Amount Per Serving): Calories **186**, Total Fat **15.5**g, Cholesterol **83**mg, Carbohydrate **11.1**g, Fiber **4.6**g, Protein **5.1**g

8-Pumpkin Pancakes

Total Time: 35 minutes

Serves: 6 pancakes

Ingredients

- 4 Tbsps. ground flax seed
- 4 Tbsps. ground hazelnuts or hazelnut flour
- 2 Tbsps. egg whites
- 1 tsp. baking powder
- 1 Tbsp. black tea (Masala Chai), powdered
- 1 tsp. of vanilla extract
- 1 cup of coconut cream
- 3 eggs
- ½ of pumpkin puree
- 5 Sweet Drops Sweetener
- 1 Tbsp. Coconut oil (for cooking)

Cooking Directions

1. Whisk together your wet ingredients for about 30 seconds, or until they become frothy.
2. In a separate bowl, mix your dry ingredients.
3. Whisk in the dry ingredients into the wet ingredient bowl. Go slow when adding in the dry ingredients. The mixture should be pourable but still thick.
4. If too thick, add in ¼ cup of water.
5. Use a teaspoon of coconut oil in a pan and ladle in your first pancake. Reduce heat to low when adding batter.
6. Cover the pan and allow the pancake to cook for 2 to 3 minutes.

7. Flip and cook the other side.
8. Serve and repeat until batter is gone.

Nutritional Value (Amount Per Serving): Calories **200**, Total Fat **17.4**g, Cholesterol **82**mg, Carbohydrate **6.4**g, Fiber **3.1**g, Protein **5.8**g

9-Keto Waffles

Total Time: 30 Minutes

Serves: 5

Ingredients

- 5 eggs, separated
- 4 Tbsps. of Coconut Flour
- 35 packets of sweetener
- 1 tsp. baking powder
- 2 tsps. of vanilla extract
- 3 Tbsps. of Full Fat Milk
- 4.5 oz. of melted butter

Cooking Directions

1. In a bowl whisk the egg whites until they are stiff and form peaks.
2. In a separate bowl combine egg yolks, coconut flour, sweetener, and baking powder.
3. Slowly mix in the melted butter until the mixture is smooth.
4. Add the milk and vanilla, and mix until smooth.
5. Fold in small amounts of the egg whites at a time; try to keep them as fluffy as possible.
6. Place the mixture into the waffle maker and cook until golden brown.

Nutritional Value (Amount Per Serving): Calories **282**, Total Fat **26.2**g, Cholesterol **219**mg, Carbohydrate **18.8**g, Fiber **9.4**g, Protein 7g

10-Spiced Granola

Total Time: 20 minutes

Serves: 4

Ingredients

- 120g of chopped pecans
- ½ cup chopped walnuts
- ½ cup of slivered almonds
- ½ cup coconut, unsweetened and flaked
- ½ cup of almond meal
- ¼ cup of flax meal (optional: or ground chia seed)
- ¼ cup pumpkin seeds
- ¼ cup sunflower seeds
- ¼ cup melted butter
- 64g of sweetener
- 1 teaspoon of honey
- 1 teaspoon of cinnamon
- 1 teaspoon of vanilla extract
- ½ teaspoon of nutmeg
- ½ teaspoon of salt
- ¼ cup of water

Cooking Directions

1. Preheat the oven to 250 degrees
2. In a large mixing bowl, mix all the ingredients. Mix them very well.
3. Place some parchment paper on a cookie sheet and grease it. Spread the granola on the paper. Place the second piece of parchment paper on top of the granola. Smooth out the

granola using a rolling pin, until it is even and firm. Remove the top parchment paper.

4.   Bake for 60 to 90 minutes or until golden brown throughout.
5.   Let cool completely before breaking into pieces and serving.

Nutritional Value (Amount Per Serving): Calories **715**, Total Fat **67.9**g, Cholesterol **31**mg, Carbohydrate **39.6**g, Fiber **22.5**g, Protein **18.2**g

Total Time: 50 minutes

Serves: 8

Ingredients

- 1 cup of whole almonds
- ½ cup macadamia nuts
- 60g pecan nuts
- 1 cup of coconut, shredded
- 1 cup of coconut, dried and flaked
- ½ cup of pumpkin seeds
- ¼ cup of Chia Seeds
- ½ scoop whey protein or powdered egg whites
- 32g of sweetener
- 4 tsp. of pumpkin spice
- ¼ tsp. salt
- ½ cup pumpkin puree
- 1 large egg
- ¼ cup coconut oil, melted and unrefined
- 15 Sweet Drops Sweetener

Cooking Directions

1. Preheat the oven to 300 degrees.
2. Roughly chop the pecans, almonds and macadamia nuts, and then place them in a mixing bowl.
3. Add coconuts, the chai and pumpkin seeds, protein, and your sweetener.
4. Add the pumpkin pie spice, eggs whites, coconut oil, and stevia. Mix until combined.

5. Mix in the pumpkin puree.
6. Place the mixture on a cookie sheet and spread out evenly.
7. Place in the oven and bake for 30 to 40 minutes. The longer you bake it the crisper it will be.
8. Let cool completely and then break up and place in an airtight container.

Nutritional Value (Amount Per Serving): Calories **382**, Total Fat **36**g, Cholesterol **27**mg, Carbohydrate **16.2**g, Fiber **8.1**g, Protein **9.2**g

12-Grain-Free Granola

Total Time: 40 minutes

Serves: 2

Ingredients

- 8 oz. of mixed nuts, unsalted (try to get one with almonds and walnuts evenly mixed)
- 42g of sweetener
- ¼ tsp. salt
- ½ tsp. of ground cinnamon
- 1 egg white

Cooking Directions

1. Preheat the oven to 350 degrees.
2. Using parchment paper, line a baking sheet with it.
3. Place the nuts into a food processer until they look like a coarse meal texture.
4. Place into a mixing bowl and add your salt, sweetener, and cinnamon. Mix well.
5. Add in the egg white and mix well again.
6. Spread the mixture on the parchment paper as thin and evenly as you can.
7. Bake for 8 to 12 minutes or until you can see some color. Make sure the nuts do not brown too much, or you will burn them.
8. Let cool completely before breaking into pieces, and store in airtight container.

Nutritional Value (Amount Per Serving): Calories **707**, Total Fat **63.7**g, Cholesterol **0**mg, Carbohydrate **50.5**g, Fiber **18.9**g, Protein **19.4**g

13-Best Avocado Breakfast

Total Time: 12

Serves: 2

Ingredients

- 4 bacon, uncured
- 1 large avocado, cut into slices and peeled
- 2 eggs
- ¼ tsp. of salt

Cooking Directions

1. Heat a pan over medium heat and place in the bacon and the avocado.
2. Flip both the avocado and bacon after 3 minutes
3. After the avocado and bacon are done set them aside. Do not clean the pan; just add in the two eggs. Fry the eggs for 2 to 3 minutes.
4. Flip eggs and cook as long as desired.

Nutritional Value (Amount Per Serving): Calories **474**, Total Fat **39.9**g, Cholesterol **205**mg, Carbohydrate **9.5**g, Fiber **6.7**g, Protein **21.5**g

Total Time: 25 minutes

Serves: 1

Ingredients

- 1 medium zucchini
- 12g of bacon
- 1 clove of garlic
- 1 Tbsp. of coconut oil
- 1 Tbsp. Chopped parsley or chives
- ¼ tsp. of salt
- 1 large egg

Cooking Directions

1. Peel and dice the onion and slice the bacon into bite-sized pieces.
2. Over medium heat sauté the onion and cook the bacon. Stir often until the onion and bacon slightly browns.
3. Dice up the zucchini into medium sized squares.
4. Add the zucchini to the onion and bacon pan. Cook for 10 to 15 minutes. Remove from heat and add the parsley.
5. Using the same pan fry an egg the way you like it and put on top.

Nutritional Value (Amount Per Serving): Calories **290**, Total Fat **24**g, Cholesterol **199**mg, Carbohydrate **8.2**g, Fiber **2.3**g, Protein **13.4**g

15-Fish and Egg Breakfast

Total Time: 15 minutes

Serves: 1

Ingredients

- 2 eggs
- 56g of Sardines in Olive Oil
- ½ cup of arugula
- 32g artichoke hearts, marinated
- A pinch of salt
- A dash of black pepper

Cooking Directions

1. Preheats the oven to 375 degrees.
2. Place the sardines in an oven ready stoneware bowl or something similar.
3. Add the eggs on top of the sardines.
4. Put the arugula and artichokes on top of the eggs.
5. Cover with the salt and pepper.
6. Bake for about 10 minutes until the eggs are how you want them.
7. Remove from oven and serve.

Nutritional Value (Amount Per Serving): Calories **258**, Total Fat **16.1**g, Cholesterol **327**mg, Carbohydrate **4.5**g, Fiber **1.9**g, Protein **13.1**g

16-Tomato Shakshuka

Total Time: 1 hour

Serves: 1

Ingredients

- 1 large yellow onion
- 1 red bell pepper
- 1.5 pounds of cherry tomatoes
- 54g extra virgin olive oil
- ½ Tbsp. of cumin seeds
- 2g of thyme, leaves picked
- 1 Tbsp. Chopped parsley
- 1 pinch of cayenne pepper
- A dash of salt
- 4 eggs

Cooking Directions

1. Preheat the oven to 350 degrees
2. Wash and cut the tomatoes in half. Place them on a lightly oiled cookie sheet.
3. Sprinkle the tomatoes with the salt.
4. Bake for 30 minutes, or until the tomatoes are roasted and look caramelized.
5. While the tomatoes bake, use a large pan and dry roast the cumin seeds for 1 minute on medium-high heat.
6. Add in the olive oil and onions, and sauté over low heat.
7. Cut the pepper into thin strips and add to the pan.
8. Add in the herbs and stir.
9. Now add the tomatoes as they come out of the oven.

10. Add a little more salt and the cayenne pepper.
11. The mixture should bubble and look juicy. If not then add a little water.
12. Add in the eggs and add them evenly to the pan.
13. Cook on low for about ten minutes, or cook until the yolk is the way you like it.
14. Serve after done cooking.

Nutritional Value (Amount Per Serving): Calories **922**, Total Fat **70.6**g, Cholesterol **655**mg, Carbohydrate **52**g, Fiber **15.1**g, Protein **31.8**g

17-Green Eggs

Total Time: 17 minutes

Serves: 2

Ingredients

- 2 Tbsps. of butter
- 1 Tbsp. of coconut oil
- 2 cloves of garlic, chopped and peeled
- 1 tsp. thyme leaves
- ½ cup chopped cilantro
- ½ cup chopped parsley
- 4 eggs
- ¼ tsp. cumin, ground
- ¼ tsp. cayenne pepper, powder
- ½ tsp. salt

Cooking Directions

1. On low heat, use a non-stick pan and melt together the butter and coconut oil for about 1 minute.
2. Add the garlic and cook on low until it begins to brown about 3 minutes.
3. Add the thyme and brown for about 30 seconds.
4. Put in the cilantro and parsley and cook on medium heat for another 3 minutes, stirring to ensure the garlic does not burn.
5. Add in the eggs; try not to break the yolks.
6. Cover the pan and return the heat to low.
7. Cook for 4 to 6 minutes.
8. Serve immediately.

Nutritional Value (Amount Per Serving): Calories **300**, Total Fat **27.4**g, Cholesterol **358**mg, Carbohydrate **3.4**g, Fiber **0.9**g, Protein **12.1**g

Total Time: 40 Minutes

Serves: 8

Ingredients

- ½ cup Almond Flour
- 1 tsp. of salt
- 1 tsp. of ground mustard
- ½ tsp. black pepper
- 1.25g of xanthan gum
- ¼ tsp. of cayenne pepper
- ¾ cup heavy cream
- 2 cups shredded cheddar cheese
- ¼ cup freshly chopped chives
- 6 large eggs, separated
- ¼ tsp. cream of tartar
- Dash of salt

Cooking Directions

1. Preheat the oven to 350 degrees. Grease 8 ramekins that can be 4 to 6 oz. Place these on a large cookie sheet.
2. In a large mixing bowl, combine almond flour, salt, mustard, pepper, xanthan gum, and cayenne. Slowly whisk in the cream until smooth. Mix the cheese, egg yolks, and chives until evenly spread.
3. In a spate, bowl beat the egg whites and combine with the cream of tartar and salt. Beat until the mixture becomes stiff and begins to show peaks.
4. Fold the egg whites into the almond flour mixture.

5. Evenly divide mixture into the 8 ramekins.
6. Place the cookie sheet and ramekins into the oven and bake for 25 minutes, or until the soufflés have risen over the rim and are golden brown.
7. Serve after pulling from the oven.

Nutritional Value (Amount Per Serving): Calories **220**, Total Fat **18.3**g, Cholesterol **185**mg, Carbohydrate **1.9**g, Fiber **0**g, Protein **12.5**g

19-Sage Breakfast Sausage

Total Time: 15 minutes

Serves: 4

Ingredients

- 1 lb. of ground pork
- 2 Tbsp. of chopped sage
- 2 packets sweetener (Swerve)
- 1 tsp. maple extract
- 1 tsp. of salt
- ½ tsp. black pepper
- ¼ tsp. of garlic powder
- ⅛ tsp. of cayenne pepper

Cooking Directions

1. Combine all ingredients in a large mixing bowl.
2. Create patties from the mixture.
3. On medium heat, place the patties onto the skillet. Cook for 3 to 4 minutes until cooked through.
4. Serve or save for later.

Nutritional Value (Amount Per Serving): Calories **170**, Total Fat **4.1**g, Cholesterol **83**mg, Carbohydrate **2.1**g, Fiber **1**g, Protein **29.9**g

20-Eggs Benedict

Total Time: 40 minutes

Serves: 6

Ingredients

- 3 eggs, separated yolks, and white
- ¼ cup Egg White Protein Powder
- ½ tsp. of dill
- 6 egg yolks
- ¼ cup of lemon juice
- 2 Tbsps. Dijon mustard
- 1½ cups melted unsalted butter
- ½ tsp. of salt
- ⅛ tsp. black pepper
- 6 ham slices
- 12 large eggs

Cooking Directions

1. For buns: preheat oven to 325 degrees. Separate the three and save the yolks. Whisk the egg whites until they are very stiff.
2. Very carefully mix in the egg white protein and dill.
3. Gently fold in the yolks you set aside, do not let the whites fall.
4. Grease a cookie sheet and place hamburger sized drops of the mixture onto the pan.
5. Bake for 20 to 30 minutes or until golden brown. Let cool completely before use.

6. For sauce: Using a double boiler, bring 1 inch of water to a simmer. Place the egg yolks, lemon juice, and mustard into the double boiler, or a small bowl of the boiler. Whisk together the mixture.
7. Continually whisk while you slowly add in the butter. Maintain the same temperature. Mix in the seasoning and whisk until thickened.
8. For poached eggs: Boil 1 inch of water in a 12-inch pan. Lower the heat to where only small bubbles appear and do not break the surface often.
9. Crack the eggs close to the water, adding them in one at a time. Do two batches so you will not overcrowd the eggs. Cook them for 3 to 4 minutes.
10. Use a slotted spoon to remove the eggs.
11. Place a slice of ham on the top of the buns, the poached eggs on the ham and 2 to 3 Tablespoons of the sauce on top of everything. Serve warm.

Nutritional Value (Amount Per Serving): Calories **294**, Total Fat **19.3**g, Cholesterol **680**mg, Carbohydrate **3.5**g, Fiber **0.6**g, Protein **25.7**g

Total Time: 5 minutes

Serves: 1

Ingredients

- 1 avocado
- 2 oz. smoked salmon
- 1 oz. Soft Goat Cheese
- 2 Tbsps. extra virgin olive oil
- 5g Juice Lemon
- A pinch of salt

Cooking Directions

1. Cut the avocado in half and remove the pit.
2. Place the remaining ingredients in a food processer and make them finely chopped.
3. Place the mixture into the avocado.
4. Eat completely or cut into pieces.

Nutritional Value (Amount Per Serving): Calories **793**, Total Fat **75.6**g, Cholesterol **26**mg, Carbohydrate **17.5**g, Fiber **13.5g**, Protein **19.4**g

22-Sausage and Cheese Muffins

Total Time: 44 minutes

Serves: 12

Ingredients

- 1 Tbsp. of olive oil
- ½ cup of chopped onion
- 1 minced clove of garlic
- 8 cups chopped Swiss chard
- 2 cups ricotta cheese
- 3 eggs
- 1 cup of shredded mozzarella
- ¼ cup of shredded parmesan
- ⅛ tsp. of nutmeg
- Salt and pepper for taste
- 1 lb. Turkey Breakfast Sausage

Cooking Directions

1. On medium heat, place the olive oil, garlic, and onions in a pan and sauté. When soft add in the Swiss chard and cook for about five minutes. The stems should be soft. Add the nutmeg, salt, and pepper. Set aside to cool.
2. In a large mixing bowl, beat the eggs. Add all the cheeses and the sautéed vegetables.
3. Press the sausage into the muffin tin, like a cupcake holder, and spoon the mixture over the sausage. Do not overfill; they will poof. Cook at 350 degrees for 30 to 35 minutes.

Nutritional Value (Amount Per Serving): Calories **178**, Total Fat **11.2**g, Cholesterol **81**mg, Carbohydrate **4.1**g, Fiber **0.5**g, Protein **16.1**g

23-Breakfast Biscuit

Total Time: 10 minutes

Serves: 1

Ingredients

- 1 oz. of cream cheese, softened
- 1 oz. of grated parmesan
- ½ tsp. of Whole Psyllium Husk
- ⅛tsp. of baking powder
- ½ tsp. of Organic Unfiltered Apple Cider Vinegar
- 1 tsp. granulated garlic
- A pinch of salt
- Black pepper
- 2 large eggs, 1 separated
- 2 Tbsps. of extra virgin olive oil
- ½ slice of American cheese

Cooking Directions

1. Blend the cream cheese, parmesan, psyllium, baking powder, vinegar, garlic, salt, and the 1 egg white. Place the batter into 2 greased 3 oz. Ramekins and place in microwave for 35 to 40 seconds, one at a time, until the center cooks through.
2. On medium heat, add olive oil to a skillet. Transfer the biscuit onto the skillet and brown both sides. Remove from skillet and top with the American cheese slice.
3. Fry your remaining eggs on the skillet and place on top of the biscuit. Serve and enjoy.

Nutritional Value (Amount Per Serving): Calories **622**, Total Fat **56.6**g, Cholesterol **432**mg, Carbohydrate **6.8**g, Fiber **1.3**g, Protein **26.2**g

Total Time: 40 minutes

Serves: 8

Ingredients

- 4 oz. of cream cheese, softened
- 1 large egg
- 2 cloves of garlic, minced
- 1 Tbsp. Chopped chives
- ½ tsp. of salt
- ½ tsp. of Italian seasoning
- 1 ½ cups of Almond Flour
- 128g of Sharp White Cheddar
- ¼ cup of heavy cream
- ¼ cup of water
- 6 oz. of Fully Cooked Sausages

Cooking Directions

1. Preheat the oven to 350 degrees
2. Whip the egg and the cream cheese using an electric mixer, on low.
3. Add the seasonings, garlic, and chives. Mix well.
4. Add in the almond flour, cheese, cream, and water. Mix until combined well.
5. Using a wooden spoon or the like, fold in the sausage.
6. Grease a muffin tin and place the dough inside.
7. Bake for 25 minutes, and let cool before removing.

Nutritional Value (Amount Per Serving): Calories **244**, Total Fat **21.3**g, Cholesterol **74**mg, Carbohydrate **3.2**g, Fiber **0.6**g, Protein **9.5**g

25-Mini Frittata

Total Time: 40 minutes

Serves: 12

Ingredients

- 8 oz. of pork sausage
- 170g Sweet Bell Peppers
- 10 eggs
- ½ cup of milk
- 2 egg whites
- ½ tsp. of salt
- ¼ tsp. of black pepper
- ½ cup of pepper jack cheese

Cooking Directions

1. Preheat your oven to 350 degrees
2. On medium heat, brown your sausage. Remove from pan and set aside.
3. Sauté peppers in the same pan.
4. In a large mixing bowl, whisk together the eggs, whites, and milk.
5. Grease a 12 spot muffin tin and divide up the sausage and peppers into each slot.
6. Evenly spread the egg mixture into the muffin tin. Use a fork to mix each one. Sprinkle with pepper jack cheese.
7. Bake for 25 to 30 minutes, should be nice, poufy, and slightly brown on top.

Nutritional Value (Amount Per Serving): Calories **150**, Total Fat **10.9**g, Cholesterol **159**mg, Carbohydrate **1.7** g, Fiber **0**g, Protein **10.7**g

26-Squash Breakfast Casserole

Total Time: 1 hour

Serves: 4

Ingredients

- 100g spaghetti squash
- 4 Tbsps. of butter
- Salt and pepper for taste
- 1 cup of diced onion
- 2 cloves of minced garlic
- ½ tsp. of Italian seasoning
- ½ cup of diced tomatoes
- 3 oz. of Classic Italian Hard Salami
- ½ cup of olives, cut in half
- 4 large eggs
- ¼ cup of parsley, roughly chopped

Cooking Directions

1. Preheat the oven to 400 degrees. Cut the spaghetti squash long ways and take out the seeds. Cover the cut side with 1 Tablespoon of butter and salt and pepper. Place in the oven to bake on a cookie sheet, cut side up, for 45 minutes, or until tender.
2. In an ovenproof skillet, melt the remaining butter on medium-low heat. Add the onions and garlic to the pan. Use the salt and pepper again for flavor. Once the onions begin to brown, add the tomatoes and salami. Cook for ten minutes before adding in the olives.
3. Add the squash to the skillet.

4. Using a spoon create four wells big enough for eggs to settle in. Crack an egg into each well. Bake in the oven until the whites of the egg are done, about 10 minutes.
5. Sprinkle with parsley and serve.

Nutritional Value (Amount Per Serving): Calories **297**, Total Fat **24.8**g, Cholesterol **236**mg, Carbohydrate **7.6**g, Fiber **1.6**g, Protein **12**g

27-Avocado Frittata

Total Time: 11 minutes

Serves: 4

Ingredients

- 4 eggs
- 10 Kalamata olives
- 2 oz. of Brie cheese (full fat)
- 1 tsp. Italian seasoning
- 2 Tbsps. of coconut oil
- ½ tsp. of salt
- 1 avocado

Cooking Directions

1. In a large mixing bowl, whisk the eggs, oil, seasonings, and olives, until the mixture becomes frothy.
2. Peel and slice the avocado into thin slices.
3. In a skillet, fry the avocado in coconut oil or spray oil. Brown both sides.
4. Remove from skillet and set aside.
5. On a high setting, pour the egg mixture into the skillet.
6. Slice the Brie into the skillet.
7. Cover and let cook for about 3 minutes.
8. Flip the frittata using the lid or a plate for assistance, and brown the top of the frittata.
9. Serve topped with the avocado.

Nutritional Value (Amount Per Serving): Calories **288**, Total Fat **26.4**g, Cholesterol **179**mg, Carbohydrate **5.5**g, Fiber **3.7**g, Protein **9.5**g

28-Pancake Donuts

Total Time: 25 minutes

Serves: 2

Ingredients

- 3 oz. of cream cheese
- 3 large eggs
- 4 Tbsps. of Almond Flour
- 1 Tbsp. of Coconut Flour
- 1 tsp. of baking powder
- 1 tsp. of vanilla extract
- 4 packets of sweetener
- 10 Sweet Drops Sweetener

Cooking Directions

1. Place all the ingredients in a blender and mix thoroughly
2. Heat up the donut maker and spray. Pour batter into each well.
3. Let cook for 3 minutes and flip, cook for 2 minutes on another side.
4. Remove from the maker and repeat until dough is gone.

Nutritional Value (Amount Per Serving): Calories **602**, Total Fat **50.9**g, Cholesterol **326**mg, Carbohydrate **21.4**g, Fiber **9.6**g, Protein **25.4**g

29-Cheddar Chive Omelet

Total Time: 15 minutes

Serves: 1

Ingredients

- 12g of bacon
- 2 large eggs
- 1 oz. of cheddar cheese
- 3g of chives, diced
- Salt and pepper for taste

Cooking Directions

1. Dice up the bacon and place in a skillet at medium heat. Cook the bacon for about five minutes. Removed from skillet and set aside.
2. Whisk the eggs, chives, salt, and pepper in a small bowl.
3. Pour the eggs mixture into the skillet still on the medium heat.
4. When the edges begin to set, add the bacon and a sprinkle of cheese to the center.
5. When the egg looks completely dry, fold over like a burrito, then flip and let cook for two minutes. Top with remaining cheese.

Nutritional Value (Amount Per Serving): Calories **323**, Total Fat **24.4**g, Cholesterol **415**mg, Carbohydrate **1.5**g, Fiber **0**g, Protein **24.2**g

30-Lemon Blueberry Muffins

Total Time: 30 minutes

Serves: 5

Ingredients

- 2 cups of Almond Flour
- 1 cup of heavy cream
- 2 eggs
- ⅛ cup of melted butter
- 5 tsps. of sweetener
- ½ tsp. baking soda
- ½ tsp. lemon extract
- ½ tsp. of dried lemon zest
- ¼ tsp. of salt
- 4 oz. of blueberries

Cooking Directions

1. Preheat the oven 350 degrees. In a 12 count muffin tin put in cup liners.
2. Mix the flour and the cream. One at a time, add the eggs. Add in the remaining ingredients except for the blueberries. Mix the ingredients until a nice mixture has formed.
3. Mix in the blueberries until they are evenly distributed.
4. Spoon the mixture into a pan, filling each holder about ½ of the way.
5. Bake for about 20 minutes or until golden brown.

Nutritional Value (Amount Per Serving): Calories **231**, Total Fat **23**g, Cholesterol **131**mg, Carbohydrate **6.2**g, Fiber **1.6**g, Protein **3**g

31-Cheesy Muffins

Total Time: 30 minutes

Serves: 12

Ingredients

- 2 cups of Almond Flour
- ½ tsp. baking soda
- ¼ tsp. of salt
- ½ tsp. of dried thyme
- 2 eggs
- 1 cup of sour cream
- ⅛ cup of melted butter
- 1 cup of Colby jack cheese
- ½ cup of Muenster cheese, shredded

Cooking Directions

1. Preheat the oven to 400 degrees and line your muffin pan with cupcake paper.
2. Whisk together all of the dry ingredients. In a separate bowl lightly beat the eggs, sour cream, and butter together. Mix the egg mixture and the flour mixture. If the batter is too thick, then add a tablespoon of water or heavy cream.
3. Add in the cheese and evenly mix. Spoon the mixture into the muffin tin, filling each spot ¾ of the way.
4. Bake at 400 degrees for 5 minutes then turn the oven down to 350 degrees. Bake the muffins for 20 more minutes. Let cool and serve.

Nutritional Value (Amount Per Serving): Calories **426**, Total Fat **39.9**g, Cholesterol **149**mg, Carbohydrate **5.5**g, Fiber **1.2**g, Protein **13.7**g

Chapter Five: Lunch

1-Bun-less Bacon Burger

Total Time: 30 minutes

Serves: 4

Ingredients

- 1½ lbs. of ground beef
- 112g pepper jack cheese
- 1 onion, cut whatever way you prefer
- 8 leaves of romaine lettuce
- Salt and pepper for taste

Cooking Directions

1. Mold your ground beef into four patties and cook on a skillet on medium heat. Cook thoroughly on both sides.
2. Cook your bacon using the same skillet until nice and crispy.
3. Using the romaine lettuce as buns sprinkle on salt and pepper and whatever condiment you would like. Melt the pepper jack cheese on the patties.
4. Place the patties on the romaine and serve.

Nutritional Value (Amount Per Serving): Calories **438**, Total Fat **19.7**g, Cholesterol **182**mg, Carbohydrate **2.9**g, Fiber **0.7**g, Protein **58.9**g

2-Chicken Salad

Total Time: 10 Minutes

Serves: 3

Ingredients

- 8g celery rib, minced
- 1 green onion, minced
- 2 Tbsps. parsley, minced
- 5 oz. roasted chicken breast, minced
- 1 egg, hard-boiled and minced
- ½ Tbsp. relish
- ⅛ tsp. granulated garlic
- ⅓ cup of mayo
- 1 tsp. Dijon mustard
- Salt and pepper

Cooking Directions

1. Place all the vegetables into a food processor and pulse them until fine. Remove into a large mixing bowl.
2. Place the chicken into the processor and pulse until fine. Transfer to mixing bowl. Do the same for the egg.
3. Add remaining ingredients and mix with a wooden spoon. Season the salad with salt and pepper, to taste.
4. Serve.

Nutritional Value (Amount Per Serving): Calories **208**, Total Fat **12**g, Cholesterol **102**mg, Carbohydrate **8**g, Fiber **0**g, Protein **17.6**g

3-Steak Salad

Total Time: 30 minutes

Serves: 4

Ingredients

- 1½ lbs. Flat Iron Steak
- ¼ cup Balsamic vinegar
- 3 Tbsps. olive oil
- 6 oz. sliced sweet onion
- 4 oz. sliced mushrooms
- 2 cloves of garlic, minced
- 1 large head of romaine, chopped
- 1 avocado, sliced and peeled
- 1 sliced orange bell pepper
- 1 sliced yellow bell pepper
- 3 oz. of sun dried tomatoes
- 1 tsp. garlic salt
- 1 tsp. onion powder
- 1 tsp. Italian seasoning
- 1 tsp. red pepper flakes

Cooking Directions

1. In a bowl, place the sliced up steak and pour the balsamic vinegar on it. Roll it around to cover the steak.
2. In a pan, heat your oil on a medium-low heat. Add mushrooms, onions, garlic, and salt and pepper, and then sauté for about 20 minutes.
3. In a mixing bowl, add romaine, tomatoes, bell peppers, and the avocado.

4. Lay the meat on a broiling pan and sprinkle with garlic salt, onion powder, Italian seasoning, and pepper flakes. Broil on high for about 5 minutes, longer if you want it cooked more.

5. Place salad mixture in a bowl and place cooked vegetables and meat on top. Serve.

Nutritional Value (Amount Per Serving): Calories **700**, Total Fat **53.1**g, Cholesterol **122**mg, Carbohydrate **31.3**g, Fiber **7.8**g, Protein **33.5**g

4-Chicken Salad with Walnuts

Total Time: 40

Serves: 6

Ingredients

- 330g Boneless And Skinless Chicken Breasts
- 1½ cups of fennel, chopped
- ¼ cup of chopped toasted walnuts
- ¼ cup of mayo
- 2 Tbsps. walnut oil
- 2 Tbsps. lemon juice
- 2 Tbsps. fennel (fronds), chopped
- 2 garlic cloves, pressed
- ⅛ tsp. cayenne pepper
- Salt and pepper for taste

Cooking Directions

1. Bake your chicken breasts at 350 for about 30 minutes. After they have cooled, dice them.
2. In a large mixing bowl mix, combine the chicken, fennel, and walnuts.
3. In a separate bowl, mix the mayo, oil, lemon juice, fennel fronds, garlic, and cayenne pepper. Whisk until smooth.
4. Pour the dressing over the salad and allow chilling in the fridge for an hour. The longer it sits the more flavors it has.

Nutritional Value (Amount Per Serving): Calories **156**, Total Fat **8.7**g, Cholesterol **34**mg, Carbohydrate **5.3**g, Fiber **1.3**g, Protein **15.1**g

5-Caesar Salad

Total Time: 15 minutes

Serves: 4

Ingredients

- 1 egg yolk
- 8 Tbsps. of avocado oil
- 3 Tbsps. apple cider vinegar
- 1 tsp. Dijon mustard
- 16g Flat Filets of Anchovies
- 2 cloves of garlic
- 28g Parmesan, grated
- 24 leaves of romaine
- 2 oz. of pork rinds, chopped
- 28g of Parmesan, shaved for the garnish

Cooking Directions

1. In a blender, place the egg yolk, apple cider vinegar, mustard. Pour the oil carefully on top of everything. Blend on low. After it resembles like mayo, add in the filets, garlic, and grated parmesan. Blend on low again until resembles mayo.
2. Arrange the romaine on four plates, drizzle with the dressing you made, top with the pork rinds and the parmesan cheese. Serve.

Nutritional Value (Amount Per Serving): Calories **196**, Total Fat **13.2**g, Cholesterol **85**mg, Carbohydrate **4.9**g, Fiber **1.3**g, Protein **15.9**g

6-Stuffed Avocado

Total Time: 5

Serves: 1

Ingredients

- 1 large avocado
- 1 can of sardines, drained
- 1 Tbsp. mayo
- 10g of chives
- 1 Tbsp. lemon juice
- ¼ tsp. turmeric powder
- ¼ tsp. salt

Cooking Directions

1. Cut the avocado in half and remove the seed. Scoop the avocado leaving ½ in to 1 inch left in the skin. In a bowl, mix the scooped avocado, chives, turmeric, and mayo. Mix well.
2. Drizzle with lemon juice on top. Place the mixture back into the avocado skin and serve.

Nutritional Value (Amount Per Serving): Calories **667**, Total Fat **54.9**g, Cholesterol **134**mg, Carbohydrate **21.9**g, Fiber **13.9**g, Protein **27.1**g

7-Chicken Salad with Pesto

Total Time: 5 minutes

Serves: 4

Ingredients

- 1 lb. of cooked chicken, cubed
- 40g slices of bacon, cooked and crispy
- 1 avocado
- 10 grape tomatoes cut in half
- ¼ cup of mayo
- 2 Tbsps. Olive Oil & Garlic Pesto

Cooking Directions

1. In a large bowl, mix all the ingredients until coated in the pesto and mayo.
2. Eat like this or add lettuce to make a bigger salad or wrap.

Nutritional Value (Amount Per Serving): Calories **503**, Total Fat **29**g, Cholesterol **105**mg, Carbohydrate **20.9**g, Fiber **7.1**g, Protein **41.6**g

8-Smoked Chicken Salad

Total Time: 1 hour 5 minutes

Serves: 4

Ingredients

- 4 cups of chicken, smoked and cubed
- 1 cup of mayo
- 1 tsp. paprika
- 1 chopped green onion
- 1 tsp. salt
- Black pepper for taste

Cooking Directions

1. Mix together mayo, paprika, and salt. Blend in the onion. Add in the chicken and mix well. Add in the pepper.
2. Chill in the fridge for 1 hour.
3. Place on salad or buns and serve.

Nutritional Value (Amount Per Serving): Calories **443**, Total Fat **23.9**g, Cholesterol **123**mg, Carbohydrate **14.6**g, Fiber **0**g, Protein **41.2**g

9-Steak Salad

Total Time: 40 minutes

Serves: 1

Ingredients

- 2 cups romaine lettuce, shredded
- ⅓ cup red cabbage, shredded
- 2 radishes, thinly sliced
- 2 Tbsps. cilantro, chopped
- 1 Tbsp. House Vinaigrette
- 3 Tbsps. Chimichurri Sauce
- 4 oz. Grilled Steak Great Salad

Cooking Directions

1. In a skillet on medium heat, cook the steaks to your preference.
2. Mix the first five ingredients. Place the steak on top and use the chimichurri sauce for dipping.

Nutritional Value (Amount Per Serving): Calories **340**, Total Fat **27.5**g, Cholesterol **32**mg, Carbohydrate **15.2**g, Fiber **2.5**g, Protein **8.3**g

10-Pesto Muffins

Total Time: 30 minutes

Serves: 5 (2-muffins each)

Ingredients

- ⅔ cup of spinach
- 3 Tbsps. pesto
- 2 oz. of olives, about
- ¼ cup of chopped sun dried tomatoes
- 5 oz. of feta cheese
- 6 large eggs
- Salt and pepper for taste

Cooking Directions

1. Preheat the oven to 350 degrees. Chop up the tomatoes. Crack the eggs into a medium sized mixing bowl.
2. Add the pesto, salt, and pepper into the mixing bowl. Divide the remaining ingredients into a greased cupcake pan. Pour the egg mixture on top.
3. Bake for 20 to 25 minutes. The muffins should appear puffy and brown on top. Remove and allow cooling before serving.
4. These will last in the fridge for up to 5 days.

Nutritional Value (Amount Per Serving): Calories **227**, Total Fat **17.9**g, Cholesterol **251**mg, Carbohydrate **4.4**g, Fiber **0.9**g, Protein **13**g

11-Quick Chicken Liver

Total Time: 5 minutes

Serves: 1

Ingredients

- 100g of chicken livers
- 3 Tbsps. butter, softened
- 1 tsp. Italian seasoning
- A pinch of salt and pepper for taste

Cooking Directions

1. Place all the ingredients in a blender and blend until a smooth paste forms.
2. Serve with crackers or radish slices.

Nutritional Value (Amount Per Serving): Calories **487**, Total Fat **42.4**g, Cholesterol **658**mg, Carbohydrate **1.5**g, Fiber **0**g, Protein **24.9**g

12-Crock Pot Chicken Chowder

Total Time: 6 hours

Serves: 4

Ingredients

- 1 lb. chicken breasts, boneless and skinless
- 8 oz. of cream cheese
- 1 cup of chicken broth
- 14 oz. of diced tomatoes
- 1 small diced onion
- 14g jalapeno, diced
- 44g lime juice
- 1 Tbsp. cilantro, chopped
- 1 clove of garlic, chopped
- 1 tsp. salt
- 1 Tbsp. black pepper

Cooking Directions

1. Combine all the ingredients into a crock-pot. Cook on high for 4 hours or on low for 6 to 9 hours.
2. When cooked shred the chicken in the crock pot using two forks and serve.

Nutritional Value (Amount Per Serving): Calories **457**, Total Fat **28.8**g, Cholesterol **163**mg, Carbohydrate **9.7**g, Fiber **2.2**g, Protein **39.7**g

Total Time: 35 minutes

Serves: 2

Ingredients

- 1 ¼ cups of shredded mozzarella cheese
- 4 Tbsps. almond flour
- 3 Tbsps. coconut flour
- 1 large egg
- 1 tsp. Italian seasoning
- 4 oz. of ham
- 3.5 oz. cheddar cheese
- Salt and pepper

Cooking Directions

1. Preheat the oven to 400 degrees. In an oven safe bowl, place the mozzarella cheese and place it in the oven until melted, about ten minutes. Stir occasionally.
2. In a small mixing bowl, combine the flours and seasonings. Mix thoroughly.
3. When the mozzarella melts, remove from oven and add the flour mixture on top. Begin to need the mixture with a wooden spoon.
4. Add the egg after the cheese has had a chance to cool. Mix in the egg until you have a workable dough. Transfer the dough to parchment paper. Place another piece of parchment paper on top and press the dough down flat with your hand. Use a rolling pin to flatten more.

5. With a pizza cutter or a knife cut diagonal lines from the top toward the middle on two sides of the dough. Do not cut all the way to the middle.
6. Layer the ham and cheese into the center of the dough. Lift one side at a time to cover the filling.
7. Bake for 15 to 20 minutes until there is a nice golden brown color. Slice up and serve.

Nutritional Value (Amount Per Serving): Calories **588**, Total Fat **38.9**g, Cholesterol **217**mg, Carbohydrate **12.5**g, Fiber **5.2**g, Protein **47.2**g

14-Mixed Greens

Total Time: 20 minutes

Serves: 1

Ingredients

- 2 oz. of mixed greens
- 3 Tbsps. of pine nuts, roasted
- 1 oz. raspberry vinaigrette
- 2 Tbsps. shaved Parmesan cheese
- 2 bacon, crispy slices
- Salt and pepper for taste

Cooking Directions

1. Cook your bacon in a skillet until nice and crispy, burned around the edges if you prefer.
2. In a shakable container add in the greens, crumble the bacon, and add the remaining ingredients. Put the lid on the container and shake well. Serve.

Nutritional Value (Amount Per Serving): Calories **447**, Total Fat **33.6**g, Cholesterol **42**mg, Carbohydrate **18.9**g, Fiber **3.5**g, Protein **19.2**g

15-Stuffed Banana Peppers

Total Time: 40 minutes

Serves: 4

Ingredients

- 4 banana peppers
- 1 lb. of Sweet Sausage
- 1 Tbsp. ghee
- ½ tsp. of Herbs de Provence
- 3 Tbsps. of yellow onions, chopped
- 125g Marinara sauce

Cooking Directions

1. Preheat the oven to 350 degrees. Slice the ends off your peppers and cut them to form boats.
2. Rub the peppers in olive oil and bake for 20 minutes.
3. While the peppers are cooking, brown your sausage in a skillet on medium-high heat. Crumble well.
4. Add in the ghee and herbs. Cook this on low for about five minutes.
5. Remove the peppers from the oven and stuff with the sausage into the peppers. Turn the broiler on high. Top the peppers with mozzarella cheese.
6. In an oven safe pan, line the bottom with the marinara sauce. Place the peppers on top and place in the oven. Cook for 5 to 10 minutes. When done the mozzarella should be bubbling and hot.
7. Cool and serve.

Nutritional Value (Amount Per Serving): Calories **392**, Total Fat **23.6**g, Cholesterol **79**mg, Carbohydrate **15.7**g, Fiber **3.5**g, Protein **22.8**g

Total Time: 10 minutes

Serves: 8

Ingredients

- 1 Tbsp. of Organic Roasted Garlic & Olive Oil
- 1 cup of Pizza Shredded Cheese Blend
- 1 cup of shredded mozzarella
- ¼ cup mascarpone cheese
- 2 Tbsps. of ghee
- 1 Tbsp. of heavy cream
- 1 tsp. of minced garlic
- ⅛ tsp. of lemon pepper
- 2 pinches of salt
- ⅓ cup of steamed broccoli
- 28g Asiago cheese, shaved

Cooking Directions

1. Heat a non-stick pan to medium heat. Add the oil and wait until it's hot. It should begin to simmer. Add in the pizza cheese and form a circle, like pizza dough. Add the mozzarella on top of this. Cook for 4 to 5 minutes until the crust is nice and crispy. Remove from pan and place on a plate to cool.
2. In the same pan, cook the mascarpone, ghee, cream, garlic, lemon pepper, and salt for another 5 minutes until it is bubbling.

3. Sprinkle the mixture over the pizza crust. Add steamed broccoli to the pan and cook. Add cooked broccoli to the pizza crust.
4. Top with the asiago cheese and serve.

Nutritional Value (Amount Per Serving): Calories **159**, Total Fat **11.9**g, Cholesterol **35**mg, Carbohydrate **2.8**g, Fiber **0**g, Protein **9.5**g

17-Bleu Bacon Zoodles

Total Time: 5 minutes

Serves: 2

Ingredients

- 4 cups of zucchini
- 1 cup of fresh spinach
- ⅓ cup of Blue Cheese dressing
- ⅓ cup crumbled Blue Cheese
- 60g of crumbled bacon, already cooked
- Black pepper for taste

Cooking Directions

1. Mix all the ingredients and enjoy.

Nutritional Value (Amount Per Serving): Calories **479**, Total Fat **40.4**g, Cholesterol **57**mg, Carbohydrate **12.5**g, Fiber **2.3**g, Protein **20.3**g

18-Cheesy Zucchini Salad

Total Time: 10 minutes

Serves: 1

Ingredients

- 2 cups of zucchini
- 1 Tbsp. of Organic Roasted Garlic & Olive Oil
- 3 Tbsps. salted butter
- 1 Tbsp. of minced garlic
- 1 tsp. of red pepper flakes
- 1 Tbsp. of chopped red pepper
- 1 Tbsp. of chopped basil
- 28g Parmesan, grated
- 28g Asiago, shaved
- Salt and pepper for taste

Cooking Directions

1. In a skillet over medium heat, melt the butter and the garlic olive oil. When melted add the garlic, pepper flakes, and red pepper, and sauté for about 1 minute. Put in the zucchini noodles and let cook for another 1 to 2 minutes. Turn off the heat and add the basil and grated parmesan.
2. Put into a serving bowl and top with the Asiago cheese. Serve.

Nutritional Value (Amount Per Serving): Calories **606**, Total Fat **49.6**g, Cholesterol **137**mg, Carbohydrate **22.3**g, Fiber **3.4**g, Protein **21**g

19-Chicken Salad Deviled Eggs

Total Time: 30 minutes

Serves: 6

Ingredients

- 6 large eggs
- 1 cup of shredded chicken
- 2 Tbsps. of mayonnaise
- 1 tsp. of Dijon mustard
- 1 Tbsp. of chopped onion
- A pinch of celery salt
- ½ tsp. of dill
- ½ tsp. of lemon pepper
- A dash of Old Bay Seasoning

Cooking Directions

1. Mix all of your ingredients except the eggs. Place in the refrigerator for later.
2. Place your eggs into a small pot. Place enough water to cover the eggs barely. Put on high heat until it begins to boil them lower to medium heat. Let boil for 15 minutes. Remove from heat and let cold water run over the eggs.
3. You will the shell off of the eggs and cut the eggs in half. Remove the yolk either throwing it away or saving it for later. Fill with your chicken salad mix that is in the refrigerator. Sprinkle the old bay seasoning on top and serve.

Nutritional Value (Amount Per Serving): Calories **128**, Total Fat **7.4**g, Cholesterol **205**mg, Carbohydrate **1.9**g, Fiber **0**g, Protein **13.2**g

20-Garlic Parmesan Wings

Total Time: 40 minutes

Serves: 2

Ingredients

- 2 Individually Frozen Chicken Wings
- 1 tsp. of garlic salt
- 2 Tbsps. of garlic oil
- 1 oz. grated Parmesan cheese
- ½ Tbsp. garlic powder

Cooking Directions

1. Preheat the oven to 450 degrees. Arrange all the wings your baking pan. Sprinkle the garlic salt on top of the wings. Cook for 35 minutes.
2. Baste with your garlic oil. Broil on high for 5 minutes until the skin is brown and crispy.
3. Remove from the oven and toss in a bowl and coat with more garlic oil. Drizzle with Parmesan and garlic powder. Serve.

Nutritional Value (Amount Per Serving): Calories **289**, Total Fat **19.1**g, Cholesterol **85**mg, Carbohydrate **5.8**g, Fiber **0.5**g, Protein **23.6**g

Total Time: 15 minutes

Serves: 2

Ingredients

- 1 lb. of Beef Shaved Steak
- ¼ cup of chopped onions
- ¼ cup of chopped green peppers
- 1 Tbsp. of minced garlic
- 1 Tbsp. of ghee
- 1 Tbsp. of olive oil
- 2 Tbsps. of mayonnaise
- 1 Tbsp. of Dijon mustard
- 4 slices of American cheese

Cooking Directions

1. In a large frying pan add the ghee and cook on medium-low heat. When melted add in the garlic, green peppers, and onions. Add the olive oil to the pan and then add the shaved steak when the oil is hot.
2. Brown the steak and then turn the heat down to low. Add in the mayo, Dijon, and mix.
3. Add the cheese on top of the steak and melt for about 1 minute. Mix thoroughly and serve.

Nutritional Value (Amount Per Serving): Calories **737**, Total Fat **53.5**g, Cholesterol **196**mg, Carbohydrate **10.5**g, Fiber **0.9**g, Protein **53.3**g

22-Pulled Lemon Pepper Chicken

Total Time: 6 hours

Serves: 4

Ingredients

- 3 lbs. of Chicken Tenderloins
- ½ stick of butter
- 1 Tbsp. of lemon pepper
- 1 Tbsp. of minced garlic
- 2 Tbsps. of olive oil
- 1 Tbsp. of salt
- 1 tsp. dried thyme
- 1 Cheddar cheese slice
- 5g Dijon mustard
- 15g Romaine lettuce or your choice of bun

Cooking Directions

1. In a crock-pot, combine the butter, lemon pepper, oil, garlic, salt, and thyme. Turn the crock-pot on high and melt the butter.
2. Place the chicken in the crock-pot; make sure to coat the chicken in the butter mixture. The batter will begin to harden.
3. Cook on high for 4 hours or on low for 6 hours. Once the chicken is done shred it in the crock-pot. Let it sit in the crock-pot for an additional 10 to 15 minutes on low.
4. Place on your chosen bun and serve.

Nutritional Value (Amount Per Serving): Calories **281**, Total Fat **21.3**g, Cholesterol **94**mg, Carbohydrate **2.2**g, Fiber **0.6**g, Protein **21.8**g

23-Cucumber Sandwich

Total Time: 5 minutes

Serves: 1

Ingredients

- ½ cup of shredded chicken
- 2 Tbsps. of pesto
- 14g of Parmesan, shredded
- ¼ chopped red pepper
- 1 cucumber cut in half and cored
- Salt and pepper for taste

Cooking Directions

1. Mix all of the ingredients together except for the cucumber.
2. Place mixture into ½ of the cucumber. Place the other half on top and eat like a sandwich.4

Nutritional Value (Amount Per Serving): Calories **340**, Total Fat **18.5**g, Cholesterol **71**mg, Carbohydrate **15.3**g, Fiber **2.7**g, Protein **30.1**g

Total Time: 10 minutes

Serves: 4

Ingredients

- ¼ cup marinara sauce
- ¼ cup shredded mozzarella
- 4 slices of salami

Cooking Directions

1. Turn your broiler on high. Place the salami on a nonstick baking sheet.
2. Put a little sauce on the salami and spread it around.
3. Sprinkle with the cheese. Cook in the oven for five minutes. Lay them on a paper towel to soak up the grease. Serve.

Nutritional Value (Amount Per Serving): Calories **94**, Total Fat **6.8**g, Cholesterol **20**mg, Carbohydrate **2.8**g, Fiber **0**g, Protein **5.2**g

25-Sausage Skillet

Total Time: 25 minutes

Serves: 2

Ingredients

- 3 sausage links
- 1 Tbsp. of white onion
- ½ cup of vodka sauce
- 28g of Parmesan cheese
- ¼ cup shredded mozzarella
- ½ tsp. of oregano
- ½ tsp. of basil
- ¼ tsp. of salt
- ¼ tsp. red pepper

Cooking Directions

1. Preheat the oven to 350 degrees. Heat up a skillet on medium heat. Add in the sausage and cook until cooked through.
2. Cut the mushrooms and onion. Remove from the skillet and use it cook the mushrooms and onion. Brown them slightly.
3. Cut the sausage into rounds and place back in the skillet. Add in the seasoning to the skillet. Pour in the vodka and the parmesan cheese. Stir and combine everything.
4. Place the skillet into the oven and let it cook for 15 minutes. A few minutes before it cooks through, sprinkle the mozzarella cheese.
5. Remove from the oven and serve.

Nutritional Value (Amount Per Serving): Calories **219**, Total Fat **14.8**g, Cholesterol **35**mg, Carbohydrate **7.7**g, Fiber **0**g, Protein **14**g

Total Time: 10

Serves: 4

Ingredients

- 3 cups of broccoli slaw
- 1 apple
- 1 tsp. of apple cider vinegar
- ½ tsp. of lemon juice
- 1 green onion
- 2 oz. of pecans
- ¼ cup mayonnaise
- ¼ cup of sour cream
- ¼ tsp. of salt

Cooking Directions

1. In a large mixing bowl, place your broccoli slaw. Shred in your apple. Chop up and place in the green onion. Chop up the pecans and add into the mix is well. Add in the remaining ingredients and mix well.

Nutritional Value (Amount Per Serving): Calories **235**, Total Fat **18.4**g, Cholesterol **10**mg, Carbohydrate **17.2**g, Fiber **4.5**g, Protein **4.2**g

Total Time: 5 minutes

Serves: 1

Ingredients

- 280g Southwest Breakfast Wrap
- 1 Tbsp. of pesto
- 280g of turkey
- 1 slice of provolone cheese

Cooking Directions

1. Spread the pesto over your wrap. Lay the Turkey on the wrap to cover about ¾ of it. Place the provolone on top of this and roll it up tightly. Cut into four or five slices.

Nutritional Value (Amount Per Serving): Calories **909**, Total Fat **39.7**g, Cholesterol **294**mg, Carbohydrate **28.2**g, Fiber **6.1**g, Protein **105.5** g

28-Mixed Salad

Total Time: 10

Serves: 1

Ingredients

- 1 cup of spinach
- 1 hard-boiled egg
- 2 Bacon Strips, cooked
- 2 oz. of chicken breast, cooked
- ½ Campari tomato
- ¼ avocado
- ½ tsp. of white vinegar
- 1 Tbsp. of olive oil

Cooking Directions

1. Shred or cut the chicken whichever way you want. Crumble the bacon. Cut the remaining ingredients into small pieces.
2. Combine all the ingredients in a bowl with the olive oil. Add dressing if you prefer.

Nutritional Value (Amount Per Serving): Calories **410**, Total Fat **27.5**g, Cholesterol **133**mg, Carbohydrate **3.6**g, Fiber **1**g, Protein **36.8**g

Total Time: 25 minutes

Serves: 8

Ingredients

- 14 eggs
- 3 plum tomatoes
- ⅔ cups of mozzarella cheese
- 42g of pepper jack cheese
- ⅓ cup of Vidalia onion
- ⅓ cup sliced jalapenos
- 5 oz. salami
- ⅓ cup of heavy cream
- 1 Tbsp. olive oil
- 1 tsp. salt
- 1 tsp. black pepper
- ½ Tbsp. cayenne pepper

Cooking Directions

1. Combine all the ingredients in a large mixing bowl. Whisk in the eggs. Mix in the cream and the cheese.
2. Pour the mixture into a greased muffin tin. Bake for 25 minutes until you begin to see a nice golden brown color.
3. Let cool for five minutes before serving.

Nutritional Value (Amount Per Serving): Calories **251**, Total Fat **18.7**g, Cholesterol **317**mg, Carbohydrate **4.8**g, Fiber **0.9**g, Protein **16.7**g

30-Cucumber Sandwich

Total Time: 5 minutes

Serves: 4

Ingredients

- 300g cucumber slices
- 4 slices (84g) Turkey Breast Meat (cold cuts)
- 2 slices of cheese cut in half

Cooking Directions

1. Peel the cucumber and slice it into eight slices.
2. Use the cucumber like bread and place the cold cuts and cheese on top of the cucumber.
3. Top with another cucumber and serve.

Nutritional Value (Amount Per Serving): Calories **90**, Total Fat **5.1**g, Cholesterol **24**mg, Carbohydrate **3.8**g, Fiber **0**g, Protein **7.6**g

Chapter Six: Dinner

1-Cheeseburger Casserole

Total Time: 45 minutes

Serves: 6

Ingredients

- 1 lb. of ground beef
- 3 Bacon Strips
- ½ cup of Almond Flour
- 360g Organic Riced Cauliflower
- 1 Tbsp. Psyllium Husk Powder
- ½ tsp. garlic powder
- ½ tsp. onion powder
- 200g Tomato Ketchup low sodium and sugar
- 1 Tbsp. Dijon mustard
- 2 Tbsps. mayo
- 3 large eggs
- 4 oz. of cheddar cheese
- Salt and pepper for taste

Cooking Directions

1. Preheat the oven to 350 degrees. Place the cauliflower in a food processor with the hamburger, bacon, and all the dry ingredients. Process the mixture until crumbly and pasty looking. Cook over medium-high heat in a skillet. Add salt and pepper.

2. Shred the cheese while you wait for the meat to cook. Place the meat in a mixing bowl with half of the cheese. Add in the mustard, ketchup, mayo, and eggs. Use a fork or your hands to mix.
3. Put into a 9 in a pan lined with parchment paper. Add the remaining cheese on top. Bake for 25 to 30 minutes.
4. Remove from oven and let stand for 5 to 10 minutes before serving.

Nutritional Value (Amount Per Serving): Calories **577**, Total Fat **31.4**g, Cholesterol **273**mg, Carbohydrate **18.2**g, Fiber **4.3**g, Protein **52.3**g

Total Time: 1 hour 5 minutes

Serves: 4

Ingredients

- 6 4-oz. Beef Short Ribs
- ¼ cup of soy sauce
- 2 Tbsps. rice vinegar
- 2 Tbsps. of fish sauce
- 1 tsp. ground ginger
- ½ tsp. onion powder
- ½ tsp. of minced garlic
- ½ tsp. red pepper flakes
- ½ tsp. sesame seed
- ¼ tsp. cardamom
- 1 Tbsp. salt

Cooking Directions

1. Combine the soy sauce vinegar and fish sauce.
2. Set the ribs in a casserole dish or a container with raised sides. Pour the marinade over the ribs and allow soaking for up to an hour.
3. Mix all the spices and seasonings. Remove the marinade from the casserole dish and sprinkle the rub over the ribs evenly.
4. Heat your grill on a medium-high heat and cook each side of the ribs for 3 to 5 minutes depending on their thickness. Serve.

Nutritional Value (Amount Per Serving): Calories **685**, Total Fat **62**g, Cholesterol **128**mg, Carbohydrate **2.5**g, Fiber **0**g, Protein **25.7**g

3-Barbeque Chicken Pizza

Total Time: 20 minutes

Serves: 4

Ingredients

- 6 large eggs
- 3 oz. Parmesan cheese
- 3 Tbsps. Psyllium Husk Powder
- 1 ½ tsp. Italian seasoning
- Salt and pepper
- 4 oz. cheddar cheese
- 6 oz. shredded chicken
- 1 Tbsp. mayo
- 4 Tbsps. BBQ sauce
- 4 Tbsps. tomato sauce

Cooking Directions

1. Preheat the oven to 425 degrees. Shred the cheese and set aside.
2. In a blender, combine the eggs, parmesan, psyllium husk powder, Italian seasoning, salt, and pepper. This dough should be thick.
3. On parchment paper, using a silicone spatula spread out the dough to fit onto a cookie sheet. Bake on the top rack for 10 minutes.
4. Flip the crust over and top with the remaining ingredients.
5. Broil for 3 minutes on high. Remove from oven and serve.

Nutritional Value (Amount Per Serving): Calories **282**, Total Fat **16.3**g, Cholesterol **239**mg, Carbohydrate **10.2**g, Fiber **3.7**g, Protein **23.9**g

4-Crock Pot Meatballs

Total Time: 2 hours 20 minutes

Serves: 6

Ingredients

- 2 lbs. of ground beef
- 1 Tbsp. of cumin
- 1 tsp. of paprika
- Salt and pepper
- 2 cups of bone broth
- 2 Tbsps. tomato paste, heaping
- ¼ cup of parsley
- 1 head of cauliflower
- ¼ cup of butter

Cooking Directions

1. Combine the meat, cumin, paprika, and salt and pepper. Mix these well and form the mixture into 1-inch balls. Line the bottom of the crock-pot with the meatballs.
2. Mix the tomato paste and the broth together. Pour over the meatballs. Slow cook for 2 hours on high or all day on the lowest setting.
3. Cut the cauliflower into florets. Steam the florets until they are soft, not mushy. Drain any extra water and place the butter and more salt and pepper on top. Throw this into a blender and blend until smooth. It will resemble mashed potatoes.
4. Place the cauliflower mash onto a plate and serve the meatballs on top.

Nutritional Value (Amount Per Serving): Calories **382**, Total Fat **17.5**g, Cholesterol **158**mg, Carbohydrate **5.7**g, Fiber **2**g, Protein **49.2**g

5-Buffalo Chicken Casserole

Total Time: 1 hour 5 minutes

Serves: 6

Ingredients

- 840g chicken thighs
- 36g of bacon
- 40g jalapenos
- 12 oz. of cream cheese
- ¼ cup of mayonnaise
- 4 oz. of shredded cheddar cheese
- 2 oz. of mozzarella cheese
- ¼ cup of hot sauce
- Salt and pepper for taste

Cooking Directions

1. Preheat the oven to 400 degrees and debone the thighs. Season your thighs with the salt and pepper. Place a sheet of tin foil on a baking sheet and place a cooling rack on top of that. Put your thighs on the cooling rack and cook for 40 minutes.
2. Halfway through the cooking, cook the chopped up bacon slices on medium heat. When it is almost done add in the jalapenos.
3. When the jalapenos are soft, add in the cream cheese and the hot sauce. Mix well and season to taste.
4. Remove the chicken from the oven and let cool. When you can touch it, remove the skins.

5. Lay the chicken in a casserole dish and cover with the cream cheese mixture. Bake this for 10 to 15. Then broil on high for 3 to 5 minutes. Let this cool for 5 minutes then serve.

Nutritional Value (Amount Per Serving): Calories **641**, Total Fat **43.9**g, Cholesterol **221**mg, Carbohydrate **5.1**g, Fiber **0**g, Protein **54.6**g

6-Chicken Nuggets

Total Time: 30 minutes

Serves: 4

Ingredients

- 24 oz. of chicken thighs
- 1 large egg
- 1.5 oz. of pork rinds
- ¼ cup of almond meal
- ¼ cup of flaxseed meal
- 67g lime, zest
- ¼ tsp. of salt
- ¼ tsp. of pepper
- ¼ tsp. of chili powder
- ¼ tsp. of paprika
- ⅛ tsp. onion powder
- ⅛ tsp. garlic powder
- ⅛ tsp. of cayenne pepper

Cooking Directions

1. Preheat the oven to 400 degrees. Pull out the chicken and pat it dry with paper towel. Cut the chicken into bite-sized pieces and set aside.
2. Combine the lime zest, spices, flax, and almond meal in a food processor. Blend until it resembles breadcrumbs. Pour this mixture into a bowl. Crack the egg into a separate bowl and whisk.

3. Dip each piece of chicken into the egg mixture then coat with the crumbs. Pace these on a baking sheet covered in tin foil. Spray the tin foil to grease it.
4. Cook these nuggets for 15 to 18 minutes. They will be golden brown on top and the meat cooks through. Serve with your favorite dipping sauce.

Nutritional Value (Amount Per Serving): Calories **480**, Total Fat **22.9**g, Cholesterol **213**mg, Carbohydrate **5.5**g, Fiber **3.3**g, Protein **60.4**g

Total Time: 1 hour

Serves: 3

Ingredients

- 1 lb. of cooked pork shoulder
- 1 Tbsp. of olive oil
- ½ tsp. jalapeno, smoke-dried and powdered
- ½ tsp. of salt
- ¼ tsp. of onion powder
- ¼ tsp. of garlic powder
- ¼ tsp. of pepper
- ¼ tsp. of oregano
- ¾ of a medium yellow bell pepper
- 14g jalapeno pepper
- 6 tortillas, flax
- 1 cup shredded romaine lettuce

Cooking Directions

1. Cut the pork shoulder into small pieces.
2. In a small bowl, mix all the spices with the oil. Pour this into a Ziploc® bag and add the pork. Roll around the bag to coat the pork. Let this sit on the counter for 30 to 45 minutes.
3. Chop the vegetables into small pieces and place them in a skillet. Add 1 tablespoon of oil to the skillet and cook on medium heat. Cook the vegetables until they are soft.
4. Add the pork mixture to the skillet and brown the pork.

5. Place the contents of the skillet into the tortillas and serve with romaine lettuce.

Nutritional Value (Amount Per Serving): Calories **602**, Total Fat **38.6**g, Cholesterol **136**mg, Carbohydrate **24.6**g, Fiber **4**g, Protein **38.5**g

8-Coconut Shrimp

Total Time: 30 minutes

Serves: 3

Ingredients

- 1 lb. of Frozen Precooked Shrimp
- 2 large egg whites
- 1 cup of Unsweetened Coconut Flake
- 2 Tbsps. of Coconut Flour

Cooking Directions

1. Thaw shrimp at room temperature. Preheat the oven to 350 degrees
2. Separate the eggs and place the egg whites into a bowl. Beat the egg whites until peaks appear.
3. In two separate bowls, place your coconut shavings and flour.
4. Dip the shrimp in the flour, egg whites, and then the coconut. Place the shrimp on a greased baking pan.
5. Bake the shrimp for about 15 minutes, the broil on high for an additional 3 to 5 minutes.

Nutritional Value (Amount Per Serving): Calories **493**, Total Fat **36.4**g, Cholesterol **151**mg, Carbohydrate **13.8**g, Fiber **12.7**g, Protein **38.1**g

Total Time: 25 minutes

Serves: 2

Ingredients

- 4 4-oz. pork loins
- 1 Tbsp. salt
- 1 Tbsp. of pepper
- 1 tsp. paprika
- 1 tsp. thyme
- ½ cup chicken broth
- ¼ cup of heavy cream
- 1 tsp. of apple cider vinegar
- 30g lemon
- 1 Tbsp. of mustard

Cooking Directions

1. Pat the pork dry and season with the thyme, paprika, pepper, and salt. In a large pan on high heat, sear the pork loins on both sides for 2 to 3 minutes. Remove from pan and set aside.
2. In the same pan, pour the chicken broth and apple cider vinegar and the heavy cream. Let this come to a simmer. Squeeze in the lemon juice and the mustard and combine.
3. Return the pork to the pan and flip in the sauce until covered. Let cook for 10 more minutes, and then serve.

Nutritional Value (Amount Per Serving): Calories **654**, Total Fat **39.4**g, Cholesterol **202**mg, Carbohydrate **7**g, Fiber **2.7**g, Protein **65.6**g

10-Sesame Chicken

Total Time: 30 minutes

Serves: 2

Ingredients

- 1 egg
- 1 Tbsp. of Arrowroot, powder
- 1 lb. of chicken thighs
- Salt and pepper
- 2 Tbsps. of soy sauce
- 1 Tbsp. of sesame seed oil
- 2 packets of sweetener (Sukrin Gold)
- 1 tablespoon of vinegar
- 1 Tbsp. of ginger
- 2 Tbsps. of sesame seeds
- 5g of xanthan gum

Cooking Directions

1. Cut the chicken into bite-sized pieces. In a bowl, combine the arrowroot and the egg. Whisk well and then place in the chicken. Cover the chicken with the mixture.
2. In a large pan heat one tablespoon of the sesame oil and add in the chicken. This should take about 10 minutes to cook.
3. In the meantime, combine all the remaining ingredients together.
4. When chicken is cooked, add the sauce and cook for another five minutes.

5. When the sauce has thickened, add the chicken on top of steamed broccoli, sprinkle with sesame seeds and green onions.

Nutritional Value (Amount Per Serving): Calories **613**, Total Fat **30.4**g, Cholesterol **284**mg, Carbohydrate **13.5**g, Fiber **4.5**g, Protein **71.4**g

11-Apple Pork Chops

Total Time: 35 minutes

Serves: 2

Ingredients

- 4 pork chops
- 2 Tbsps. of olive oil
- Salt and pepper for taste
- 2g Paprika
- ½ apple
- 3g of rosemary
- 2 Tbsps. apple cider vinegar
- 1 Tbsp. of lemon juice
- 1 Tbsp. of maple syrup
- 2 Tbsps. of olive oil

Cooking Directions

1. In a 400-degree oven heat up a large cast iron skillet.
2. While waiting on the skillet prep your pork chops. Pat them dry with paper towels. Then rub down with the olive oil and dry seasonings.
3. Remove the skillet from the oven and place on the stove on high heat. Sear your pork chops on each side for 2 minutes.
4. Place the slices of apple and rosemary on top of the pork. Place back in the oven and cook for an additional ten minutes. Make your vinaigrette while waiting.
5. Combine the remaining ingredients together, adding the oil last. Whisk it in slowly.
6. Top with the vinaigrette and serve.

Nutritional Value (Amount Per Serving): Calories **815**, Total Fat **68.3**g, Cholesterol **138**mg, Carbohydrate **14.8**g, Fiber **2.1**g, Protein **36.4**g

12-Pan Seared Salmon

Total Time: 40 minutes

Serves: 2

Ingredients

- 1 Tbsp. of olive oil
- 2 cloves of garlic
- ½ lb. of mushroom
- 2 Tbsps. of butter
- 75g Campari tomatoes
- 2 cups of spinach
- Salt and pepper for taste
- 1 Tbsp. of balsamic vinegar
- 2 4-oz. Salmon Filet

Cooking Directions

1. Pat you filets dry getting rid of any excess moisture. Season both sides of the filets with salt and pepper. Place in the fridge while you are prepping the rest of the recipe.
2. On medium heat, heat some of the olive oil. Add slices of garlic, mushrooms, and tomatoes. When the vegetables have shrunk, add in the butter to make them crispy. Add in your spinach and cook until wilted. Remove from the pan onto a plate and cover with foil.
3. Heat up the remaining amount of olive oil. Wait until the oil is very hot. Lay the salmon filets on the pan skin side down, let sear for 4 to 5 minutes. Flip them to the other side and cook for another 4 to 5 minutes.

4. Drizzle your balsamic vinegar over the vegetables and place the salmon on top. Serve.

Nutritional Value (Amount Per Serving): Calories **367**, Total Fat **26**g, Cholesterol **91**mg, Carbohydrate **7.4**g, Fiber **2.4**g, Protein **27.3**g

13-Beef Stir Fry

Total Time: 40 minutes

Serves: 2

Ingredients

- 2 Tbsps. sesame seed oil
- 2 garlic cloves
- 1 tsp. of ginger
- 1 carrot
- ¼ medium red onion
- 1 zucchini
- 14g jalapeno
- 1 lb. of beef
- ½ tsp. of salt
- pinch of pepper
- ¼ tsp. of red pepper flakes
- ¼ tsp. of Chinese 5 spice
- ¼ cup of beef broth
- ¼ cup of coconut milk
- 1 oz. of cashews
- 6g of fresh basil

Cooking Directions

1. Chop up all of your vegetables and set aside. In a pan, heat 1 tablespoon of sesame oil on medium heat. Throw in your garlic, onion, carrots, and ginger and cook until they are fragrant. If the garlic browns, turn down the heat.
2. Add in your jalapenos and zucchinis as well as the seasonings. Combine by tossing and set aside on a plate.

Slice of your beef into thin strips. Warm the other tablespoon of sesame oil and place in the pan. Brown both sides of your beef. When the beef is done, put the veggies back into the pan. Pour in your beef broth and the coconut milk.

3. Add in your cashew nuts and let cook for 8 minutes uncovered. Add in your basil and cook for another five minutes before serving.

Nutritional Value (Amount Per Serving): Calories **742**, Total Fat **42**g, Cholesterol **203**mg, Carbohydrate **16.2**g, Fiber **3.7**g, Protein **74.4**g

Total Time: 35 minutes

Serves: 2

Ingredients

- 3 sausage links
- 1 tablespoon of white onion
- 4 ounces of mushrooms
- ½ cup of vodka sauce
- 28g of Parmesan cheese
- ¼ cup of shredded mozzarella
- ½ teaspoon of oregano
- ½ teaspoon of basil
- ¼ teaspoon of salt
- ¼ teaspoon of red pepper

Cooking Directions

1. Preheat the oven to 350 degrees. Heat a cast iron skillet on medium heat until it is close to smoking. Add in the sausage and cook until almost done.
2. Slice up your mushrooms and onion while the sausage is cooking. When the sausage is almost done, remove it from the pan and throw in the mushrooms and onion, browning them for a bit.
3. Cut the sausage into rounds and return then to the pan. Season the mixture with the spices. Pour the vodka sauce and cheese. Stir and combine everything.
4. Place the skillet in the oven to cook for 15 minutes. Sprinkle mozzarella to melt. Pull from the oven and serve.

Nutritional Value (Amount Per Serving): Calories **231**, Total Fat **15**g, Cholesterol **35**mg, Carbohydrate **9.6**g, Fiber **0.8**g, Protein **15.8**g

Total Time: 30 minutes

Serves: 2

Ingredients

- 300g of chicken (wings, drums)
- ½ cup of hot sauce
- 2 Tbsp. of butter
- Salt and pepper
- 3g garlic powder
- 1 tsp. paprika
- 2g cayenne pepper (optional)

Cooking Directions

1. Break your chicken wings into 2 pieces and discard the tips. Pour enough of the hot sauce into the wings to coat them. Season your wings and place them in the fridge for 1 hour (this is optional if you are in a hurry.
2. Turn your broiler on high. Line a baking sheet with foil and place the wings on it so they are not touching. Broil the wings for 8 minutes.
3. While the wings are cooking in a pan, melt the butter and the rest of the hot sauce. Sprinkle with cayenne pepper, if desired. Flip the wings when they are done and cook for another 8 minutes.
4. When the wings are crispy, place them in a mixing bowl and pour the hot sauce mixture on them. Toss them to spread the sauce evenly.

Nutritional Value (Amount Per Serving): Calories **346**, Total Fat **16.6**g, Cholesterol **146**mg, Carbohydrate **3.3**g, Fiber **1**g, Protein **44.4**g

16-Chicken Kiev

Total Time: 50 minutes

Serves: 2

Ingredients

- 12 oz. chicken breasts
- 4 Tbsp. of butter
- 2 cloves of garlic
- 5g of green onion
- 2g tarragon leaves
- 1 Tbsp. parsley
- Salt and pepper
- 1 oz. of pork rinds
- 1 egg
- ¼ cup of Coconut Flour

Cooking Directions

1. Preheat the oven to 350 degrees. Pound the chicken until it is about 1 cm thick. Season it with the tarragon, parsley, salt, and pepper. Cut the butter into strips that will fit along the chicken. Add the chopped onion and garlic on top of this.
2. Roll the chicken up and pin using toothpicks.
3. Turn your pork rinds into breadcrumbs by blending them. Pour into a bowl. Place your flour in another bowl. In another bowl, whisk your egg.
4. Coat your chicken in the flour, making sure to cover every part. Then dip in the egg, then the rinds.

5. Fry your chicken in a well-oiled pan on medium heat. All sides should be equally crisp. Remove from the pan and place in a safe oven container. Place in the oven and cook for 20 minutes. Pull out of the oven and serve.

Nutritional Value (Amount Per Serving): Calories **718**, Total Fat **45.5**g, Cholesterol **315**mg, Carbohydrate **11**g, Fiber **6.3**g, Protein **64.9**g

17-Cheddar Chicken Casserole

Total Time: 55 minutes

Serves: 6

Ingredients

- 20 oz. of chicken breasts
- 2 Tbsps. of olive oil
- 2 cups of broccoli
- ½ cup of sour cream
- ½ cup of heavy cream
- 1 cup of cheddar cheese
- 1 oz. of pork rinds
- Salt and pepper
- ½ tsp. of paprika
- 1 tsp. of oregano

Cooking Directions

1. Preheat the oven to 450 degrees. If using fresh broccoli steam it for a few minutes to help soften it.
2. Cook the chicken in a pan until cooked all the way through. Shred it in the pan.
3. In a mixing bowl, combine the broccoli, chicken, oil, and sour cream. Place this mixture into an 8 x11 pan. Spread evenly and press firmly. Drizzle with heavy cream over the casserole. Add all of your seasonings and sprinkle the cheese on top. Crush up the pork rinds and sprinkle them on top. Place in the oven and bake for 20 to 25 minutes. The edges will be brown, and the casserole will be bubbling when done.

Nutritional Value (Amount Per Serving): Calories **410**, Total Fat **27.5**g, Cholesterol **133**mg, Carbohydrate **3.6**g, Fiber **1**g, Protein **36.8**g

Total Time: 40 minutes

Serves: 6

Ingredients

- 1 Tbsp. of olive oil
- 20 oz. of chicken breast
- 2½ oz. of mushrooms
- ¼ cup of mayonnaise
- 2 cups cauliflower, riced
- ¼ cup of heavy cream
- 1 cup of chicken stock
- ½ cup of vodka sauce
- 1 cup of mozzarella cheese
- 1 oz. of pork rinds
- 56g of Parmesan cheese
- Salt and pepper
- 1 tsp. Oregano
- 1 tsp. Garlic powder

Cooking Directions

1. Preheat the oven to 375 degrees. Rice the cauliflower until you have 2 cups. Put it in a pot with boiling chicken broth and cook for 10 to 15 minutes until the liquid evaporates. evaporated. In a pan, cook your chicken breasts all the way through. Shred them with two forks. Add the heavy cream to your cauliflower and cook for an additional 5 minutes.
2. Slice up the mushrooms and combine with chicken and mayonnaise. Add in the cauliflower and use the seasonings.

Add in your vodka sauce and combine well. Put the mixture into a baking dish into a nice even layer.

3. Top with the cheeses and your pork rinds and cook for 20 minutes or until the casserole is bubbling.

Nutritional Value (Amount Per Serving): Calories **374**, Total Fat **18.9**g, Cholesterol **115**mg, Carbohydrate **8.1**g, Fiber **1.1**g, Protein **44**g

19-Slow Cooked Chuck Steak

Total Time: 8 hours

Serves: 8

Ingredients

- 4.4 pounds of chuck steak
- 3 carrots
- 4 celery stalks
- 1 cup of red wine
- 2 cloves of garlic
- 2 cups of beef stock
- Salt and pepper

Cooking Directions

1. Place your roast into the slow cooker with 1 inch of water. Cook on high for 4 hours.
2. After the steak has been cooking for 4 hours slice up the vegetables and place around the roast. Pour the broth and the wine over the roast. Season with the salt and pepper and whatever other spices you would like. Allow to cook for four more hours.
3. Cut the steak and serve with the vegetables.

Nutritional Value (Amount Per Serving): Calories **667**, Total Fat **32.8**g, Cholesterol **264**mg, Carbohydrate **3.6**g, Fiber **0.7**g, Protein **78.5**g

20-Cabbage Salad

Total Time: 30 minutes

Serves: 6

Ingredients

- 1 head of cabbage
- 1 stick of butter
- ½ cup of water
- 1 ½ pounds of ground beef
- 2 cups of marinara sauce
- 2 cups of cheddar cheese
- 56g Parmesan cheese

Cooking Directions

1. Peel off the outside of the cabbage. Cut the cabbage into sections so it will fit into a food processor. When done it will be fine strips.
2. In a pan, melt the stick of butter. Then add in the water and the cabbage. Cook for about 12 minutes.
3. In a separate pan, brown the ground beef. Drain the beef when cooked and add in with the cabbage. Add in the marinara sauce and mix. Add the cheese on top and mix.
4. Serve in a bowl topped with parmesan cheese

Nutritional Value (Amount Per Serving): Calories **630**, Total Fat **39.2**g, Cholesterol **190**mg, Carbohydrate **119.2**g, Fiber **5.2**g, Protein **49.9**g

Total Time: 2 hour

Serves: 8

Ingredients

- 1 brown onion
- 8 garlic cloves
- 3 eggplants
- 1 zucchini
- 7 oz. of diced tomatoes
- 7 oz. tomato paste
- 1.1 pounds of ground beef
- ¼ cup of red wine
- 8 tablespoons of butter
- 2 eggs
- 1 cup of heavy cream
- 56g of Parmesan

Cooking Directions

1. Finley dice your onion and peel the eggplants and zucchini. Cut up the eggplants and the zucchini into small strips. Set into a colander for later.
2. Take 2 tablespoons of butter and melt in a pan on low heat. Put the onions in the pan and cover them in the butter. When the onions begin to brown, add the garlic and allow it to cook for 10 minutes. Add in the ground beef and keep on the same heat.
3. When the beef cooks up, add the tomatoes and the tomato paste. Mix in well and add in the spices.

4. Wash your eggplants and zucchini. In a medium sized pan, heat oil on medium heat and fry the vegetables on both sides, and begin to layer them in an oven safe dish. Layer the meat sauce on top and create three layers.

5. In another pot, melt and mix the remaining butter with parmesan cheese. Add in the cream and mix again. Let cool until you can touch it. Whisk the eggs together in a bowl when the cheese is cool. Pour this mixture on top of your meat vegetable layers.

6. Heat your oven to 355 degrees. Cook for 30 minutes, but check every ten minutes. It will be a nice brown on top when done. Let cool before serving.

Nutritional Value (Amount Per Serving): Calories **404**, Total Fat **24.2**g, Cholesterol **153**mg, Carbohydrate **21.8**g, Fiber **9.2**g, Protein **26.9**g

22-Burger Boats

Total Time: 40 minutes

Serves: 4

Ingredients

- 2 pounds of ground beef
- Seasoning salt
- Romaine lettuce leaves
- 1 red bell peppers
- ½ of Avocado
- 14g Jalapenos
- 32g Combo Pack (Ketchup and Mustard)

Cooking Directions

1. In a mixing bowl, put in the ground beef and seasonings. Mix it with your hands to event blend. Make patties that will fit onto your lettuce. Set aside.
2. In a pan melt some butter and slice the pepper into large strips. Add it to the pan and fry them until soft. Remove the peppers and set aside.
3. Using the same pan and cook your patties to your liking.
4. Create your boats. Start with the lettuce and add a couple peppers. Place your patty on top and top that with the avocado, jalapenos, ketchup and mustard. Serve.

Nutritional Value (Amount Per Serving): Calories **483**, Total Fat **19.1**g, Cholesterol **203**mg, Carbohydrate **4.2**g, Fiber **2.4g**, Protein **69.6**g

23-Bacon Stir Fry

Total Time: 10 minutes

Serves: 3

Ingredients

- 5 Bacon Strips
- 3 cups of mixed vegetables, frozen
- 1 Tbsp. soy sauce

Cooking Directions

1. Cut the bacon into small pieces. In a pan, start cooking the bacon on high heat. Add in the vegetables and cook until everything is soft.
2. Add the soy sauce and stir thoroughly.
3. Serve.

Nutritional Value (Amount Per Serving): Calories **258**, Total Fat **15.6**g, Cholesterol **0**mg, Carbohydrate **17.9**g, Fiber **9.3**g, Protein **10.5**g

Total Time: 20 minutes

Serves: 4

Ingredients

- 1 lb. of ground beef
- 1 tsp. Italian seasoning
- 1 Tbsp. of butter
- 2 Tbsps. of minced garlic
- 2 cups of marinara sauce
- 2 cups spaghetti squash

Cooking Directions

1. In a pan on medium heat, brown the beef. Add in the butter, seasoning, and garlic. Mix and cook for another 2 minutes.
2. Add in the marinara sauce and mix. Place the spaghetti squash on a plate and cover with the sauce. Serve.

Nutritional Value (Amount Per Serving): Calories **370**, Total Fat **14**g, Cholesterol **112**mg, Carbohydrate **22.2**g, Fiber **3.3**g, Protein **37.2**g

Total Time: 45 minutes

Serves: 6

Ingredients

- 1 8 oz. of mozzarella cheese
- 2 pound of flank steak
- 340g of spinach (bunch)

Cooking Directions

1. Preheat the oven to 350 degrees. Shred the mozzarella cheese in a food processor. Slice your steak, so it is nice and square, removing any hard fats as well. Beat it thin.
2. Line the steak with the cheese and the spinach, and then roll up. Tie the steak with cooking twine and season with Italian seasoning.
3. Line a 9x9 pan with spinach. Cut the steak into six rounds and place on top of the spinach. Try to have a string on each round.
4. Bake for 25 minutes or until done enough for you.

Nutritional Value (Amount Per Serving): Calories **414**, Total Fat **19.5**g, Cholesterol **103**mg, Carbohydrate **3.4**g, Fiber **1.2**g, Protein **54.5**g

Total Time: 1 hour 15 minutes

Serves: 4

Ingredients

- 3 Tbsps. Sunflower Seed Butter
- 2 tsp. of hot sauce
- 1 Tbsp. of soy sauce
- 1 Tbsp. of minced garlic
- ½ tsp. of crushed red pepper
- 1 Tbsp. of water
- 1 lb. of pork (kebab), squared
- 1 medium green pepper

Cooking Directions

1. In a blender or food processor mix together the butter, hot sauce, soy sauce, garlic, red pepper, and water. Cut your pork into squares and place in a bowl. Pour the marinade over the pork and let sit for 1 hour.
2. Chop the pepper into small pieces but not too small, they need to fit on the skewer.
3. Thread the pepper and pork onto the skewers. Place on a baking sheet and broil on high for 5 minutes on each side.

Nutritional Value (Amount Per Serving): Calories **242**, Total Fat **8.6**g, Cholesterol **83**mg, Carbohydrate **5.5**g, Fiber **2.2**g, Protein **33.7**g

27-Sausage Wrapped in Bacon

Total Time: 10 minutes

Serves: 4

Ingredients

- 450g Italian sausages
- 190g of bacon, sliced

Cooking Directions

1. Preheat a deep fryer to 370 degrees. If no deep fryer place a good amount of oil in a pan and heat on high heat.
2. Cut the sausages into 4 pieces. Cut the bacon in half. Wrap the sausage in the bacon and skewer the bacon in place. Fry in the oil for 3 to 4 minutes until crispy.

Nutritional Value (Amount Per Serving): Calories **646**, Total Fat **55.1**g, Cholesterol **138**mg, Carbohydrate **1.4**g, Fiber **0**g, Protein **33.6**g

Total Time: 4 hours 40 minutes

Serves: 4

Ingredients

- 2 racks St. Louis Style BBQ Ribs
- 1 Tbsp. of paprika
- 2 Tbsps. of Splenda
- 1 Tbsp. of garlic powder
- 1 Tbsp. of salt
- ½ Tbsp. of pepper
- ½ Tbsp. of ground ginger
- ½ Tbsp. of onion powder
- ¼ Tbsp. cayenne pepper
- 2 oz. of Dijon mustard

Cooking Directions

1. Preheat the oven to 225 degrees. If the ribs have a membrane on the back, remove it.
2. In a small bowl mix together all of the spices.
3. Spread the mustard all over the ribs. Rub the spices all over the ribs.
4. Line a baking sheet with baking foil. Place the rib on the sheet and bake uncovered for 1 hour.
5. Make a tent of foil over the meat and cook for 3 ½ more hours. Turn the ribs after 2 hours.
6. Remove the foil and broil for 5 minutes. Cover and let rest for 10 minutes before serving.

Nutritional Value (Amount Per Serving): Calories **355**, Total Fat **19.4**g, Cholesterol **0**mg, Carbohydrate **27.6**g, Fiber **2.3**g, Protein **17.5**g

29-Fried Pork Chops

Total Time: 10 minutes

Serves: 3

Ingredients

- 3 pork chops
- ½ cup of Coconut Flour
- 1 tsp. of seasoned salt
- 1 tsp. of black pepper
- 1 Tbsp. of butter

Cooking Directions

1. In a large bowl mix together all the dry ingredients. Pat dry the pork chops.
2. Heat up a skillet on high heat and melt the butter.
3. Coat the pork chops in the dry ingredient mix and add to the heated pan. Cook each side for 4 to 5 minutes.

Nutritional Value (Amount Per Serving): Calories **385**, Total Fat **27.1**g, Cholesterol **79**mg, Carbohydrate **12.4**g, Fiber **8.2**g, Protein **22.1**g

30-Chicken Spaghetti

Total Time: 20 minutes

Serves: 4

Ingredients

- 5 oz. of spinach
- 12 oz. of chicken (leftover)
- 14 oz. spaghetti squash
- 1 Tbsp. minced garlic
- 4 oz. of cream cheese
- 1 oz. of grated Parmesan cheese

Cooking Directions

1. Dice up your leftover chicken. Drain your spinach and heat the spaghetti squash.
2. Heat some bacon in a cast iron skillet. Add in the squash and spinach. Add in the chicken.
3. Mix in the cream cheese and parmesan cheese. Top with a little extra parmesan and serve.

Nutritional Value (Amount Per Serving): Calories **292**, Total Fat **14.7**g, Cholesterol **102**mg, Carbohydrate **9.8**g, Fiber **0.8**g, Protein **30.9**g

Chapter Seven: Soup

1-Chili

Total Time: 1 hour 15 minutes

Serves: 6

Ingredients

- 1¼ lbs. of ground beef
- 8 oz. tomato paste
- 1½ chopped tomatoes
- 1 chopped red bell pepper
- ½ cup chopped onion
- 40g celery, chopped
- 1½ tsps. of cumin
- 1½ tsps. chili powder
- ½ tsp. black pepper
- 1½ tsp. salt
- ¾ cup of water (more if you need it)

Cooking Directions

1. Brown the meat in a skillet. When cooked sprinkle with salt. Add the pepper and onions to the pan and cook for 2 minutes on medium heat.
2. In a large pot combine all the ingredients and bring to a boil.
3. Lower the heat to low-medium and let the chili simmer for 1 to 2 hours. Stir every 30 minutes or so to keep it from sticking.

Nutritional Value (Amount Per Serving): Calories **228**, Total Fat **6.4**g, Cholesterol **84**mg, Carbohydrate **11.3**g, Fiber **3**g, Protein **31.1**g

2-Mexican Chicken Soup

Total Time: 4 hours 5 minutes

Serves: 6

Ingredients

- 1½ lbs. of boneless skinless chicken
- 15.5 oz. chunky salsa
- 15 oz. chicken broth
- 8 oz. Monterey or pepper jack cheese

Cooking Directions

1. Line the bottom of your crock pot with the chicken. Add the rest of the ingredients on top.
2. Cook for 3 to 4 hours on high, or 6 to 8 hours on low.
3. When done shred the chicken in the pot.
4. Serve the dish hot.

Nutritional Value (Amount Per Serving): Calories **395**, Total Fat **21.1**g, Cholesterol **141**mg, Carbohydrate **4.8**g, Fiber **1.2**g, Protein **44.8**g

3-Veggie Soup

Total Time: 20 minutes

Serves: 6

Ingredients

- 1 medium Cauliflower heads
- 1 medium onion
- 2 cloves of garlic
- 1g crumbled bay leaf
- 150g Watercress
- 200g fresh spinach
- 4 (100g) of vegetable stock
- 1 cup cream or coconut milk
- ¼ cup of coconut oil
- 1 tsp. of salt and pepper for taste

Cooking Directions

1. Peel and dice the garlic in the onion. Cook in a soup pot with coconut oil over medium-high heat. Cook until slightly brown. Wash watercress and spinach and set aside.
2. Cut the cauliflower into florets and place in the pot with the onion and garlic. Add the bay leaf and cook for 5 minutes. Mix frequently.
3. Add in your spinach and watercress and cook for 3 minutes.
4. Pour in the vegetable stock and bring the pot to a boil. Cook this into a cauliflower is crisp. Add in the cream.
5. Season assume salt and pepper. Take a hand blender and blend until the soup is creamy. You can serve hot or chill it.

Nutritional Value (Amount Per Serving): Calories **156**, Total Fat **11.7**g, Cholesterol **8**mg, Carbohydrate **10.5**g, Fiber **3.9**g, Protein **4.6**g

4-Kielbasa Cabbage Soup

Total Time: 30 minutes

Serves: 6

Ingredients

- 6 bacons, chopped
- 1 lb. of Kielbasa, sliced
- 6 cups chopped cabbage
- ¼ cup chopped onion
- 1 tsp, salt
- ½ tsp. black pepper
- 3 cloves of garlic, minced
- 1 tsp. thyme
- 6 cups of chicken broth
- 28 g Parmesan, grated for garnish

Cooking Directions

1. Cook the bacon in a stockpot on medium heat. When crispy remove and set aside.
2. Add the sliced kielbasa and sauté until browned. Add in the onion and cabbage, frequently stirring, for about 4 minutes, or until they have softened. Add the salt, pepper, thyme, and garlic, cooking this mixture for another minute.
3. Pour in the chicken broth and bring to a simmer. The cabbage needs to be tender. Simmer for about 10 minutes.
4. Serve with the parmesan grated on top.

Nutritional Value (Amount Per Serving): Calories **350**, Total Fat **23.7**g, Cholesterol **77**mg, Carbohydrate **9.5**g, Fiber **2**g, Protein **24.4**g

5-Chicken Noodle Soup

Total Time: 1 hour 30 minutes

Serves: 4

Ingredients

- 4 cups of chicken broth
- 1 lb. of chicken, cooked and shredded
- 1 cup chopped celery
- 1 cup chopped yellow squash
- 2 cups chopped zucchini
- 1 cup chopped onion
- ½ cup chopped green beans
- 1 tsp. of basil
- 1 tsp. of salt
- Black pepper for taste

Cooking Directions

1. In a large pot combine all of the ingredients and add water if needed.
2. On high heat, bring that to a boil. When boiling and reduce the heat and cover, let simmer for 90 minutes.
3. Serve with pepper for taste.

Nutritional Value (Amount Per Serving): Calories **243**, Total Fat **5**g, Cholesterol **87**mg, Carbohydrate **8.2**g, Fiber **2.4**g, Protein **39.5**g

Total Time: 6 hours

Serves: 6

Ingredients

- 14 oz. Beef Smoked Sausage
- 32 oz. of beef stock
- 12 oz. Regular Bottle Beer
- 1 cup of chopped carrots
- 1 cup of chopped celery
- 1 small diced onion
- 4 minced garlic cloves
- 1 tsp. red pepper flakes
- 1 tsp. salt
- ½ tsp. of black pepper
- 1 cup of heavy cream
- 8 oz. of cream cheese

Cooking Directions

1. In a slow cooker, put in the sausage, stock, beer, celery, carrots, onion, pepper flakes, garlic, salt, and pepper. Cook this on high for 4 hours.
2. Add the remaining ingredients and whisk together until there are no more lumps. Cook for another 2 hours.

Nutritional Value (Amount Per Serving): Calories **892,** Total Fat **48.9**g, Cholesterol **144**mg, Carbohydrate **34**g, Fiber **2.3**g, Protein **23.9**g

7-Broccoli Soup

Total Time: 10 minutes

Serves: 4

Ingredients

- ¼ cup of heavy cream
- ¼ cup of cream cheese
- ¼ cup of sour cream
- ¼ cup of almond milk
- 4 oz. of cheddar cheese
- 1 cup (91g) of steamed broccoli
- ½ of Onions
- ½ of a chicken bouillon cube

Cooking Directions

1. Steam your chopped broccoli florets, takes about 3 minutes in the microwave. Place a little bowl of water in with the broccoli.
2. Add the liquid ingredients into a blender. Add in the broccoli, onion, and cheese. Break up the bouillon cube and sprinkle on top.
3. Mix on a soup setting and serve once nice and creamy.

Nutritional Value (Amount Per Serving): Calories **270**, Total Fat **24**g, Cholesterol **62**mg, Carbohydrate **5.3**g, Fiber **1.2**g, Protein **10**g

Total Time: 3 hours 50 minutes

Serves: 8

Ingredients

- 4 lbs. of chicken thighs, boneless skinless
- 1 lb. of chorizo
- 4 cups of chicken stock
- 1 cup of heavy cream
- 14 oz. of tomatoes, stewed
- 2 Tbsps. of minced garlic
- 2 Tbsps. of Worcestershire sauce
- 2 Tbsps. hot sauce
- Sour cream and Parmesan, for garnish

Cooking Directions

1. Brown the chorizo in a skillet on medium heat.
2. Lay the ingredients in the crock-pot starting with the chicken and chorizo.
3. Cook for 3 hour on high. Remove the thighs and return to the pot. Cook for 30 minutes on low.
4. Use the garnish and serve.

Nutritional Value (Amount Per Serving): Calories **762**, Total Fat **44.5**g, Cholesterol **272**mg, Carbohydrate **5.3**g, Fiber **0.7**g, Protein **80.5**g

9-Chicken Chili

Total Time: 6 hours 5 minutes

Serves: 8

Ingredients

- 2 Tbsps. of butter
- 1 onion
- 1 pepper
- 800g chicken thighs, boneless
- 48g of bacon
- 1 Tbsp. of thyme
- 1 tsp. of salt
- 1 tsp. of pepper
- 1 Tbsp. of minced garlic
- 1 Tbsp. of Coconut Flour
- 3 Tbsps. of lemon juice
- 1 cup of chicken stock
- ¼ cup of unsweetened coconut milk
- 3 Tbsps. of tomato paste

Cooking Directions

1. Place the butter on the bottom of a crock pot and allow to melt on low heat. Thinly slice the vegetables and evenly place them in the pot.
2. Place the chicken on top of the vegetables. Add the seasoning. Pour on the liquids and tomato paste and cook on low for 6 hours.
3. Stir everything and break up the chicken before serving.

Nutritional Value (Amount Per Serving): Calories **285**, Total Fat **14.9**g, Cholesterol **103**mg, Carbohydrate **4.4**g, Fiber **1.3**g, Protein **32.2**g

10-Shrimp Stew

Total Time: 20 minutes

Serves: 6

Ingredients

- 1½ pounds of raw shrimp, peeled and deveined
- ¼ cup of olive oil
- ¼ cup of diced onion
- 1 clove of garlic, minced
- ¼ cup red pepper, roasted, diced
- ¼ cup cilantro, chopped
- 14 oz. can tomatoes, diced
- 1 cup of coconut milk
- 2 tablespoon hot sauce
- 30g lime juice
- Salt and pepper

Cooking Directions

1. In a medium pan, heat up the oil on medium heat. Throw in the onions; cook until transparent. Add the peppers and garlic, cook for 3 minutes more. Add in the tomatoes, shrimp, and cilantro. Let that simmer until the shrimp turns opaque.
2. Pour in the coconut milk and hot sauce. Do not boil, just cook until heated. Add in the lime and salt and pepper for seasoning.

Nutritional Value (Amount Per Serving): Calories **319**, Total Fat **19.9**g, Cholesterol **239**mg, Carbohydrate **8.7**g, Fiber **2.2**g, Protein **27.5**g

11-Tomato Soup

Total Time: 5 minutes

Serves: 4

Ingredients

- 4 Roma tomatoes
- ½ cup of sun dried tomatoes
- ½ cup of macadamia nuts
- 1 tsp. of salt
- ¼ cup of basil
- ½ tsp. of white pepper
- ¼ tsp. of black pepper
- 1 clove of garlic
- 4 cups of hot water

Cooking Directions

1. Add all the ingredients to a blender and blend on high for five minutes. Serve.

Nutritional Value (Amount Per Serving): Calories **174**, Total Fat **14.9**g, Cholesterol **0**mg, Carbohydrate **10.8**g, Fiber **3.9**g, Protein **3.2**g

1-Mozzarella Bites

Total Time: 15 minutes

Serves: 3

Ingredients

- ⅓ cup panko (herb flavored)
- 3 (21g) Cheddar sticks
- 2 egg whites
- ¼ cup marinara sauce

Cooking Directions

1. Preheat the oven to 425.
2. In a medium skillet, cook the panko on medium heat until toasted, about 2 minutes. Make sure to stir the whole time. Remove from the skillet and place in a bowl. Place the egg whites into a separate bowl.
3. Cut the cheese into 1-inch pieces. One at a time dip the cheese into the egg and then roll in the panko. Place the cheese on a greased baking sheet.
4. Bake for 3 minutes. Heat the marinara sauce in the microwave for 30 seconds, or until heated.

Nutritional Value (Amount Per Serving): Calories **157**, Total Fat **8.2**g, Cholesterol **20**mg, Carbohydrate **11.7**g, Fiber **1.1**g, Protein **9.4**g

2-Turkey Roll-up

Total Time: 2 minutes

Serves: 1

Ingredients

- 1 oz. turkey, roasted and sliced
- 1 oz. (28g) Cheese

Cooking Directions

1. Cut the cheese into a long strip that fit in your turkey.
2. Wrap the turkey around the cheese and eat.

Nutritional Value (Amount Per Serving): Calories **162**, Total Fat **10.8**g, Cholesterol **51**mg, Carbohydrate **0.4**g, Fiber **0**g, Protein **15.4**g

3-Raspberry Popsicles

Total Time: 2 hours

Serves: 6

Ingredients

- 100g of raspberries
- 24 g lemon juice
- ¼ cup of coconut oil
- 1 cup of coconut milk
- ¼ cup of sour cream
- ¼ cup of heavy cream
- 6g guar gum
- 20 Sweet Drops Sweetener

Cooking Directions

1. Mix all the ingredients in a blender then pour into Popsicle molds. Freeze for at least 2 hours.

Nutritional Value (Amount Per Serving): Calories **221**, Total Fat **22.6**g, Cholesterol **11**mg, Carbohydrate **5.8**g, Fiber **2.8**g, Protein **1.6**g

4-Dried Fruit Mix

Total Time: 1 minute

Serves: 1

Ingredients

- Dried apricots
- Dried kiwi
- Dried Strawberries
- Raisins

Cooking Directions

1. You can pick any dried fruit you want in your mix, make sure to check the sugar content to keep it low.
2. If you have a dehydrator, you can make your own dried fruit and keep the ingredients in check.

Nutritional Value (Amount Per Serving): Calories **145**, Total Fat **0.8**g, Cholesterol **0**mg, Carbohydrate **36.5**g, Fiber **4.2**g, Protein **2.2**g

5-No Bake Bombs

Total Time: 25 Minutes

Serves: 8

Ingredients

- ½ cup of coconut oil
- ¼ cup of cocoa powder
- 4 (31g) scoops protein powder
- 6 (100g) servings of Shelled Hemp Seeds
- 2 Tbsps. of heavy cream
- 1 tsp. of vanilla extract
- 28 Sweet Drops Sweetener
- ¼ cup of unsweetened coconut, shredded

Cooking Directions

1. Mix the dry ingredients with the coconut oil until it becomes a paste.
2. Add in the cream, vanilla, and stevia. Mix again until it becomes creamy.
3. Place the coconut on a plate. Roll out balls using your hands and roll in the coconut. Place on a baking sheet with parchment paper on it. Freeze the balls for 20 minutes.

Nutritional Value (Amount Per Serving): Calories **652**, Total Fat **54.3**g, Cholesterol **37**mg, Carbohydrate **9.6**g, Fiber **5.5**g, Protein **38.1**g

6-Flaxseed Chips

Total Time: 10 minutes

Serves: 36

Ingredients

- 6 shells (360g) Flaxseed Tortillas
- 3 Tbsps. of olive oil
- 1 tsp. (2g) Salt and pepper

Cooking Directions

1. Cut the tortillas into chip-sized cuts.
2. Place into the oil heated on medium-high heat. Cook until crispy. Remove from oil and place on a paper towel. Season the chips with salt and pepper, to taste. Repeat with the rest of the chips.

Nutritional Value (Amount Per Serving): Calories35, Total Fat1.9g, Cholesterol 0mg, Carbohydrate 4.5g, Fiber 0.8g, Protein 0.8g

7-Corndog Bites

Total Time: 20 minutes

Serves: 20

Ingredients

- ½ cup of Almond Flour
- ½ cup of flaxseed meal
- 1 Tbsp. of Psyllium Husk Powder
- 3 packets (6g) sweetener
- ¼ tsp. of salt
- ¼ tsp. baking powder
- ¼ cup of melted butter
- 1 large egg
- ⅓ cup of sour cream
- ¼ cup of coconut milk
- 10 (57g) Little Smokies

Cooking Directions

1. Preheat the oven to 375 degrees. Mix all the dry ingredients into a bowl. Add the egg, sour cream, and butter to this and mix well. Once mixed add in the coconut milk.
2. Grease a 20 mini muffin pan and place in the batter.
3. Cut the Smokies in half and press into the center of the batter in each muffin.
4. Bake for 12 minutes and then broil on high for 1 to 2 minutes. Cool before removing from the tin.

Nutritional Value (Amount Per Serving): Calories **149**, Total Fat **13.8**g, Cholesterol **35**mg, Carbohydrate **2.5**g, Fiber **1.4**g, Protein **4.2**g

8-Peanut Butter Log

Total Time: 5 minutes

Serves: 1

Ingredients

- 4 Tbsps. of peanut butter
- 2 stalks of celery

Cooking Directions

1. Cut the celery in half, and line with the peanut butter. If desired, you can line with raisins as well.

Nutritional Value (Amount Per Serving): Calories **381**, Total Fat **32.3**g, Cholesterol **0**mg, Carbohydrate **13.6**g, Fiber **4.3**g, Protein **16.2**g

9-Cucumber Chips

Total Time: 3 minutes

Serves: 1

Ingredients

- 1 cucumber

Cooking Directions

1. Slice the cucumber into rounds. Eat plain or in a dip.

Nutritional Value (Amount Per Serving): Calories **45**, Total Fat **0.3**g, Cholesterol **0**mg, Carbohydrate**10.9**g, Fiber**1.5**g, Protein **2**g

10-Veggie Dip

Total Time: 5 minutes

Serves: 1

Ingredients

- 6 Baby carrots
- 1 broccoli head, cut into florets
- 1 cauliflower head, cut into florets
- Ranch dressing

Cooking Directions

1. Cut up the broccoli and the cauliflower. Pour the ranch into a bowl.
2. Dip the vegetables and enjoy.

Nutritional Value (Amount Per Serving): Calories **127**, Total Fat **0.7**g, Cholesterol **0**mg, Carbohydrate **25**g, Fiber **10.8**g, Protein **8.6**g

11-Nut Mix

Total Time: 5 minutes

Serves: 1

Ingredients

- 10 pieces (14g) pecans
- ¼ cup walnut, shelled
- ¼ cup almonds

Cooking Directions

1. Mix all the nuts together and enjoy.

Nutritional Value (Amount Per Serving): Calories **428**, Total Fat **40.3**g, Cholesterol **0**mg, Carbohydrate **10.2**g, Fiber **6.6**g, Protein **14**g

Chapter Nine: Drinks

1-Coconut Chocolate Smoothie

Total Time: 10 minutes

Serves: 1

Ingredients

- ¼ cup coconut milk
- 2 Tbsps. Coconut Butter
- 1 Tbsp. coconut oil
- 1 Tbsp. unsweetened cocoa powder
- 1 scoop (34g) whey protein, unflavored
- 1 packet (2g) sweetener
- ½ cup water
- ½ cup of ice

Cooking Directions

1. Place all the ingredients into a blender and blend until smooth.
2. Pour into a glass and enjoy.

Nutritional Value (Amount Per Serving): Calories **608**, Total Fat **50.5**g, Cholesterol **65**mg, Carbohydrate **19.9**g, Fiber **8.1**g, Protein **26.6**g

2-Berry Smoothie

Total Time: 10 minutes

Serves: 1

Ingredients

- ⅓ cup heavy whipping cream
- ½ cup water
- ½ cup almond milk
- ½ cup blackberries or strawberries, frozen
- 1 Tbsp. coconut oil
- 1 tsp. vanilla extract
- 1 packet (2g) sweetener

Cooking Directions

1. Blend all the ingredients in a blender until smooth.
2. Serve in a glass

Nutritional Value (Amount Per Serving): Calories **574**, Total Fat **57.4**g, Cholesterol **55**mg, Carbohydrate **17.2**g, Fiber **7.5**g, Protein **4.6**g

3-Almond Butter Smoothie

Total Time: 10 minutes

Serves: 1

Ingredients

- 1 scoop (41g) Vanilla Protein Powder
- 4 Tbsps. heavy cream
- 2 Tbsps. Smooth Almond Butter
- 1 packet (2g) sweetener
- ½ cup water
- ½ cup ice

Cooking Directions

1. Blend all the ingredients until smooth.
2. Serve in a glass.

Nutritional Value (Amount Per Serving): Calories **547**, Total Fat **41.7**g, Cholesterol **142**mg, Carbohydrate **20.7**g, Fiber **6**g, Protein **30.2**g

4-Coffee Smoothie

Total Time: 10 minutes

Serves: 1

Ingredients

- 1 packet (2g) sweetener
- 3 oz. coffee (cold)
- ¼ tsp. vanilla extract
- ½ tsp. cinnamon
- 3 Tbsps. heavy cream
- 1 Tbsp. unsweetened cocoa powder
- 1 cup of ice

Cooking Directions

1. Place all the ingredients in a blender and blend until smooth.
2. Top with whip cream and chocolate sauce is preferred.

Nutritional Value (Amount Per Serving): Calories **174**, Total Fat **17.4**g, Cholesterol **62**mg, Carbohydrate **7.2**g, Fiber **3.4**g, Protein **2.1**g

5-Avocado Smoothie

Total Time: 10 minutes

Serves: 1

Ingredients

- ½ avocado
- ½ cup almond milk
- ¼ cup cream
- 1 tsp. cinnamon
- 2 Tbsps. coffee creamer (vanilla)
- 1 Tbsp. almond butter (unsweetened)
- A dash of sugar for taste
- ½ cup of ice

Cooking Directions

1. Place all ingredients into the blender and blend until smooth.
2. Serve and enjoy.

Nutritional Value (Amount Per Serving): Calories **687**, Total Fat **66.4**g, Cholesterol **31**mg, Carbohydrate **23.4**g, Fiber **11.2**g, Protein **9.4**g

6-Peppermint Smoothie

Total Time: 10 minutes

Serves: 1

Ingredients

- 1 cup cashew or almond milk
- 1 scoop of chocolate whey protein
- ¼ tsp. mint extract
- A handful of spinach
- A handful of ice

Cooking Directions

1. Blend all the ingredients.
2. Pour in a glass and serve.

Nutritional Value (Amount Per Serving): Calories **913**, Total Fat **65.5**g, Cholesterol **65**mg, Carbohydrate **49.6**g, Fiber **4.8**g, Protein **44**g

7-Peanut Butter Smoothie

Total Time: 10 minutes

Serves: 1

Ingredients

- 1 scoop whey protein (chocolate)
- 1 cup water
- ⅓ cup (40g) heavy cream
- 3 ice
- 2 tablespoons peanut butter

Cooking Directions

1. Blend all the ingredients together until nice and smooth.
2. Serve in a glass.

Nutritional Value (Amount Per Serving): Calories **446**, Total Fat **32.8**g, Cholesterol **119**mg, Carbohydrate **11.1**g, Fiber **1.9**g, Protein **31**g

8-Strawberry Smoothie

Total Time: 10 minutes

Serves: 1

Ingredients

- 1 cup coconut milk (unsweetened)
- 5 strawberries, frozen
- 2 Tbsps. heavy cream
- 1 Tbsp. sage
- 1 Tbsp. vanilla syrup, sugar free

Cooking Directions

1. Blend all the ingredients until smooth. Serve.

Nutritional Value (Amount Per Serving): Calories **721,** Total Fat **68.8**g, Cholesterol **41**mg, Carbohydrate **30.5**g, Fiber **7.3**g, Protein **6.7**g

9-Raspberry Smoothie

Total Time: 10 minutes

Serves: 1

Ingredients

- 1 cup of almond milk
- ½ cup of raspberries
- 1 oz. of cream cheese
- 1 Tbsp. of vanilla syrup

Cooking Directions

1. Blend all the ingredients and serve.

Nutritional Value (Amount Per Serving): Calories**723,** Total Fat **67.5**g, Cholesterol **31**mg, Carbohydrate **31.9**g, Fiber **9.3**g, Protein **8.4**g

10-Strawberries Smoothie

Total Time: 10 minutes

Serves: 1

Ingredients

- 5 strawberries
- 3 Tbsps. of heavy cream
- 1 Tbsp. vanilla syrup

Cooking Directions

1. Blend together all the ingredients until smooth. Serve in a glass.

Nutritional Value (Amount Per Serving): Calories **214**, Total Fat **16.8**g, Cholesterol **62**mg, Carbohydrate**16.4**g, Fiber **1.2**g, Protein **1.3**g

11-Orange Chocolate Smoothie

Total Time: 10 minutes

Serves: 1

Ingredients

- 1 cup of almond milk
- 1 scoop whey protein (chocolate powder)
- ⅛ tsp. of orange (extract)
- 1 cup spinach
- 3 ice

Cooking Directions

1. Blend all the ingredients and serve.

Nutritional Value (Amount Per Serving): Calories **679**, Total Fat **59.2**g, Cholesterol **65**mg, Carbohydrate**18.1**g, Fiber **6**g, Protein **28.5**g

Conclusion

First off all I wanted to thank you for taking the time to read this book and learn about the ketogenic diet. For many people changing their mindset on the way they eat is a very hard thing to accomplish and with the information and the meals that we have presented you with today it is our hopes that you can start to change and se results.

From this point forward it will be your job to start developing your own meal plans, finding new and innovative recipes to try and take your ketogenic experience to the next level. In this book we have walked you through the basics and given you the tools needed for success. What you do with them from here is the next big question.

As someone who struggles with weight themselves I know how hard it is to fight temptations and gravitate towards the not so good for your body. With the ketogenic diet you get the best of both worlds as well as the knowledge and tools needed for success.

And to know that you are not along. There are many people out there struggling as well. If you find yourself struggling, go ahead and seek out these support groups and communities that can be of support and guidance towards your end goals.

-V.I.P Invitation-

Green Protein VIP

In order for us to further assist you, we invite you to

Join Green Protein VIP

Join Green Protein VIP today and gain access to our exclusive **Healthy Life Easy: 104 Juicing Recipes For Weight Loss** book for **Free**, which contains 104 healthy juicing recipes that will cleanse your body, help you loss weight and feel better overall!

In addition, you will have access to the following as a VIP member:

* Discover Exclusive Deals & Discover Before Anyone Else!

* Be The First to Know About Green Protein's Hot New Releases!

* Get Free Exclusive Cookbooks, Dieting Books, and Recipe Journals by Green Protein

* And Much Tastier Recipes and Advices to Better Guide You On Your Journey

Go To https://greenprotein.leadpages.co/healthy-nation-vip/ now to join and enjoy your 3rd Free Book!

You can learn more about your 3rd Free Book on the Next page

Made in the USA
San Bernardino, CA
28 February 2018

Within this book you will receive 104 Tasty Juicing Recipes that can be made easily to go along with your healthy meals. Each recipe also has everything you need to know such as: serving, prep time, and most importantly nutritional values. So, we can help you to keep track of your healthy lifestyle.

Click on the Image or go to
https://greenprotein.leadpages.co/healthy-nation-vip/ to get your free copy now!